African Igloos and Public Service Heroes

African Igloos
and
Public Service Heroes

Peter Latchford

WingFast

Published by
Wingfast Publishing Ltd
Buxton House
All Stretton
Shropshire SY6 6JS
www.wingfast.biz

ISBN 978-0-9566235-0-8

British Library Cataloguing in Publication Data.
A catalogue record for this book is available from the British Library.

Typeset in 11.5pt Garamond by Troubador Publishing Ltd, Leicester, UK
Printed the UK by TJ International Ltd, Padstow, Cornwall

Peter Latchford

Peter Latchford has infiltrated the public sector and lived to tell the tale. He has been Chair, Chief Executive and troubleshooter in a variety of public service organisations, in health, housing, regeneration, community cohesion, enterprise, infrastructure, local authority, museums, skills, business support, and crime.

Peter is a Director of Black Radley Ltd, the fairness and effectiveness specialist. His writing on public sector solutions has been published widely in the mainstream and specialist press. He is a visiting Professor of Enterprise at Birmingham City University, Chair of Urban Living (the housing market renewal pathfinder), Chair of a LIFTCo (a public-private partnership in the health sector), Vice Chair of the Community Development Foundation, and Fellow of the RSA.

CONTENTS

INTRODUCTION

HEROISM AND THE FALL FROM GRACE

For most of those not involved, and for many of those who are, public service is seen as rule bound, inefficient and impersonal. An object of derision. A drain on the economy. A laughable demonstration of politicians' inability to manage anything. A burden unwillingly carried by the average tax payer.

It shouldn't be. It should be glorious, rewarding, honourable. A vocation. Something to be aspired to. A good way to spend a life.

Public service should be, and should be seen to be, a way to build the competitiveness of our economy and to develop the moral and social fabric of our nation. It should be a fair, personal, responsive force which supports and protects all of our people.

But it isn't. Why not? Because we allowed it to fall from grace. Because we have, systematically, thoroughly, with our eyes open, over an extended period of time, screwed all the life out of it. We have blocked public servants who wanted to be enterprising. We have suppressed them when they wanted to take risks. We have sneered when they tried out new ideas.

We have worked hard to stop people getting things done.

We have been hounded by a hostile and derisive media. This has made us run in terror from risk – into the arms of the greatest danger of all: that of having meaningless lives. It has cowed us into thinking that government money is someone else's, not our own. It has tainted the name of enterprise – because enterprise sounds as if it is about business, which it is, of course, and therefore profit, which it does not have to be. It has made us uncomfortable about people making money from public service.

Liberating enterprise

There are good people in public service doing good work in spite of the way things are. We must liberate them. We must overturn the systems, find new and better ways of doing things and allow public servants to be moral agents whose fundamental job is to engage with the citizen.

We must bring enterprise back to public service. Enterprise as a way of thinking at the policy level. Enterprise as problem solving at the coal face. Enterprise as a way of working, a personal disposition. Because real enterprise – the unashamed desire to get things done – is a quality that must be admired, not stamped out.

This book is a call to arms to the potential public sector hero; to enterprising people; to people who hunt down problems so that they can solve them.

Problems, problems

The public sector is full of problems. If we work in public service – as a nurse, a skills broker, an unemployment advisor, a manager, a senior civil servant, a councillor, a Member of Parliament – we know that problems are stock in trade.

If we do not work in public service, the media reminds us of these problems every day, sneering at the shortcomings of government programmes, mocking targets missed, ignoring successes achieved – judging public servants (politicians and employees) by standards most of us could never hit. Politicians rail against this. Civil servants become risk averse. But the problems and the attendant publicity remain.

This is unsurprising: the fundamental role of the public sector is to solve health, education, housing, defence, economic, and social problems. And the problems in these areas are themselves problematic: they are complex, shifting, inter-related and hard to engage. The public sector, from policy making through to implementation, is about problems. It is there to identify and resolve problems. Not all of them will ever be solved. But it is the duty of any civilised people to seek ways to do so. And it is the duty of the media to hold the problem solvers to account.

Counter-productive approaches

Unfortunately, much that we do in the public sector is unnecessary, ineffective, or straightforwardly counter-productive. We have good intentions but lousy strategies and half hearted tactics. Partly as a result, we have ended up with an overblown public sector industriously perpetuating itself through departments, agencies and contracts; through partnerships, strategies and consultancy assignments; through anaemic elections, unaccountable appointees and hierarchical employment practices.

This book is based in part on my own experience of public sector leadership. More significantly, it is built on the access I have had to a wide range of excellent leaders and front line folk during the last decade when I worked as a public sector troubleshooter. Though I have borrowed shamelessly from their wisdom and advice, any shortcomings or inadequacies in what I have to say are entirely my own.

PART ONE

WHERE THE TROUBLE COMES FROM

The UK public sector is enormous. Around 40% of the country's income from economic activity is spent by the government. Approximately 20% of people in work are employed in public service. The sector has been growing for most of the last century.

On the one hand, the way in which a society looks after its underprivileged is a mark of its humanity. Public spending, if it is about anything, is surely about helping those that need help. We know that too great a gap between the richest and the poorest causes all kinds of social tensions which benefit no-one's long term wellbeing.

On the other hand, too big a public sector can create too great a weight on the economy. It may burden the wealth generators with an expensive and inflexible overhead which constrains their flexibility and competitiveness.

Only elected politicians can and should answer the question: What should the public sector do? Their answers must take into account:

- economic and social considerations
- the balance of interests across the population
- moral imperatives concerning minority and disadvantaged groups

- trade-offs between the long and short term.

This is not a political book. But we can say this. **The public sector spends too much.** How do we know? Because the analysis and regulation to which most public sector organisations are subject consistently demonstrate that they are often less than fully effective and usually inefficient. So, wherever the line is drawn between what should and should not be paid for by the public purse, we know that what is being paid is too much for what is being delivered.

The ineffectiveness disease

In public service it is hard to get things done.

- The UK public sector is large, multi-layered and inter-dependent.
- There is complexity of service, organisation, and systems.
- Risk aversion is endemic.
- Politicians and managers tinker with structures, success measures and contracts.

They may have little political choice, but their best intentions mostly miss the point: they address systems, not the situation on the ground. We all know on a personal basis that results are achieved through people – through energy and networks – not through dry systems and structures. If you want something done, you do not think, "What process do I follow?" You think, "Who do I know that knows how to do this?" Yet public sector management is devoted to systems, structures and processes. The sector regularly goes through paroxysms of restructuring. Every 8 to 10 years, agencies or departments that had been decentralised are centralised, and agencies that were centralised are decentralised. The rationale is pretty consistent: driven by a perception of under performance, ministers and senior management argue that centralisation will lead to savings from economies of scale; or that decentralisation will lead to greater customer responsiveness.

In practice, such benefits are rarely achieved. Typically, *the trauma caused by redundancies and disturbance to systems and relationships outweighs the planned benefits.* So much effort is put in to managing the structural change that little management time can be spared to ensure that services are properly tailored and responsive to individual clients.

'They' should do something!

The popularity of such structural change is explained by our over-emphasis on targets and 'strong leadership'. Senior managers who restructure look as if they are doing something assertive and purposeful: they can point to the restructure as evidence of the efficiencies they are achieving, or the customer-responsiveness they are constructing. They certainly generate considerable managerial activity: planning, change management, job evaluations, redundancies, recruitment, and training. But, though this may be rewarding for managers at all levels, it rarely has much to do with either customer service or efficiency. *The real job of management is to get results.*

How? By getting close to the operational front line. By supporting it in providing excellent and flexible service to the end client. Yes, it's grimy and it's compromised. Yes, it calls for rolled up sleeves and attention to detail. And, let's not shirk this, it's a lot less sexy than planning and implementing structural change. So: what does it mean to get things done in the public sector? When all the titles, rhetoric, strategies and memos are stripped away, what is it all about?

There are essentially two requirements for delivering effective public service. These are:

1. avoiding abuse of the public purse
2. releasing enterprise in staff.

There is a necessary tension between these two requirements. Good public sector management is about achieving the right balance. Too often, though, public sector practice is concerned with the first to the exclusion of the second. Control tools suffocate empowerment and enterprise. Usually, these control tools are selected simply because nobody realises there are alternatives – or because the alternatives look too unpleasant or brutal.

The standard control tools are:

- detailed written procedures for all activities within the department or agency
- tightly specified contracts between the department/agency and its deliverers
- a hierarchy of targets by which staff performance is reviewed
- a hierarchical reporting structure.

There is an underlying belief system behind the use of these control tools. It declares that:

- desired outcomes can predictably be achieved if certain activities are undertaken
- these activities can be specified and planned in advance
- the core management issue is simply to ensure that the units of work (staff or contractors) conform to the pre-specified rules of engagement – and that, if they do so, all will be well.

In practice, since public service is usually about service, not manufacturing, the connections between plans, procedures, activities and results are much looser. Even in a manufacturing environment some of these control tools have lost their allure.

In most public service environments, the good work that is achieved is done despite, not because of, such controls.

In control or uninvolved?

The logic of the standard approach may be intellectually compelling but is almost always problematic on the ground. Targets are rendered irrelevant by changed circumstances. Procedures are rendered inappropriate by new challenges because they fail to allow for unforeseen and inappropriate shortcuts. Many public service managers spend a good deal of their time attempting to design, re-design or 'roll out' such control tools. In practice, this means that their time is spent in meetings with their peers, in meetings with other levels of the hierarchy, in meetings with HR, in sessions reviewing staff performance, and at the computer re-mapping or redrafting procedures, flow charts and contracts. All of which leaves very little time for *getting out of the office and overseeing how well the job is actually being done.*

The Golden Thread
The Golden Thread philosophy of target-setting within an organisation is seductive. This approach advocates the development of a hierarchy of targets aligned with the hierarchy of management where each person knows what they should be achieving and how it contributes to the overall organisational objectives.

The problem is that, in reality, for the public sector, the approach usually does not work. Jane has missed her targets by a mile for well understood reasons beyond her control – but has clearly done extremely useful work. Bob has exceeded his targets as a result of unexpected economic shifts, but is clearly lazy and incompetent.

The gap between contracts and delivery
There are big problems in the contract management of suppliers. Public

sector contract paperwork has a tendency to swell as contract managers try to close potential loopholes and disseminate to all areas what has been identified, in a specific case, as good practice. The consequence of this is that both sides are forced to pour increasing resources into the management of the contract interface so as to demonstrate bureaucratic (output) conformance on the one hand, and expert supervision on the other. This leaves less resource for delivery and for monitoring real achievement.

In addition, a commissioning department or agency looking to demonstrate its efficiency and show headcount reduction will typically reduce its number of contract managers. The consequence of this, to ensure that the remaining contract managers are not overloaded, is usually to move to fewer, larger contracts. But the activity levels remain the same, thus leading to a lack of contract control, since there are fewer contract managers to oversee it.

And in procurement the over-emphasis on control also has curious and counter-productive results. In the UK we are (rightly) anxious, at the policy level, to avoid nepotistic or old boy network practices in public spending. Procurement has to be effected through a transparent and objective process.

This good intention results in:

1. a highly specified, and therefore laborious, bidding process
2. disinclination, amongst contract managers and procurement officers, to take any risks in choice of supplier.

And the consequence of this is that only bigger businesses can afford to invest the time it takes to bid for contracts, and only the biggest businesses win them – since nobody ever got sacked for buying from a business everyone else is buying from. But the biggest businesses are the least easy for any one contract manager to control since no one contract is as important to them as it would be to a smaller operator.

The fundamental intent – to be fair and objective in the selection of contractors – is undermined by the very practices that are supposed to fulfil it.

Many good managers understand and are frustrated by the overall state of affairs. It can seem that there are no alternatives. What has happened is that there is an imbalance between, on the one hand, enabling staff or contracting agencies to achieve and, on the other hand, safeguards to ensure that public funds are properly spent. *The control orientation has overwhelmed the enterprise imperative.* This has happened in part because of our collective cold fear of risk-taking with public funds, and because of the over-use of certain control tools.

The value of enterprise

Enterprise is a positive concept. It is an attribute most people would rather have applied to them than not. Governments want it, big business wants it, we all want it. But, like love, another positive concept, it can mean all things to all people. And it can be very hard to get, especially when you try too hard.

Enterprise is not just about entrepreneurs. Entrepreneurs, usually taken to mean people who start businesses, are not the only people who are enterprising. Single parents on low income who have to feed their children and stay sane are enterprising. Children may be enterprising in the way they overcome homework problems. This is an important distinction, since supporting enterprise is fundamentally important to economic, social and individual health, whereas commercial entrepreneurship – though important – simply cannot be managed.

Very few people can be successful commercial entrepreneurs, just as very few people can win 100m Olympic sprint medals or be leading Hollywood actors. For a fourteen year-old about to set out on their path through adult life, it is statistically not worth trying to be a successful entrepreneur. There are simply too many factors beyond one individual's control to allow for any certainty of making it happen. Less than one per cent of people who set out on this course succeed. That is not to say that people should not try – just as we should not say that people should not try to succeed in film or to be an Olympic sprint champion. But being a commercial entrepreneur is not a **career** option. And a government policy of supporting entrepreneurs is certainly not worth pursuing to exclusion of all else.

Financial wealth or a meaningful life?

It has become increasingly clear in recent years, as the number of truly wealthy people in the developed world has grown, that high levels of wealth are not worth having. Financial security up to a certain point is of value in reducing stress, improving heath, and increasing happiness. But beyond that quite low level, wealth becomes a problem, a factor in a range of personal and family problems.

The underlying reason is straightforward: as humans, **we are meaning-oriented**. We gain our sense of self from striving towards something. When there is nothing to strive towards, there is no meaning and no pleasure. Life should be a work of art – what else is there? Being an enterprising person, being a person who gets things done – now, *that* is fulfilling. Being a commercial entrepreneur – a person who makes money – may or may not provide fulfilment depending on the level of enterprise involved.

But much individual dreaming is muddled on this score. Much public policy development (government dreaming) is also confused. What an economy needs is enterprise. What governments often pursue are commercial entrepreneurs, but these embody only one (quite rare) type of enterprise. At the heart of the problem is the perception that both enterprise and entrepreneurship are about getting rich quick. In reality, **enterprise is about getting things done**. According to this definition of enterprise, it may or may not lead on to riches. It is almost certain, however, that it will lead to **life wealth**. And, properly supported, it leads to economic and social strength.

A further misconception is that enterprise is about taking **risks**. This is understandable, since the risks associated with doing something are typically more obvious than those associated with doing nothing. But passive risks are often greater than active risks. Active risk taking can lead to unexpected positive results. If you try, you may fail. But if you fail, you meet people, learn things, gain a sense of self – and, in so doing, put yourself in a stronger position to succeed next time. Who lives longer, the couch potato or the athlete? We need enterprising people in the public as well as the private sector.

We need them as relatives, friends, artists, entertainers and community leaders, too.

Plans, Plans, Plans!

In the mid 1990s, Tom Barker was appointed Chief Executive of one of the new Business Links, support agencies for small businesses set up and funded by central government. With a background in small manufacturing – he had run his family automotive components business until his customers started sourcing from abroad – Tom felt pretty sure he understood the tough conditions faced by the small business owner.

Central government had identified a problem – a market problem – with support for small business. The UK economy relies on businesses, the vast majority of which are small, most of which are performing well below their potential. Business owners are unwilling to pay for the advice and support which would make them significantly more effective and profitable. A relatively small investment by the government in encouraging and subsidising business advice ought, therefore, to pay handsome returns to the economy and the exchequer.

On his first day Tom had no staff, no systems, no support – just an office, a telephone and an indicative budget. It felt like an exciting opportunity to get the thing right. One of his first actions was to get hold of a copy of the government contract and read it through carefully to discover what his civil servant contract managers wanted.

As he read and re-read, what dawned on Tom, schooled as he was in a world where what works is much more important than what might look like a good idea, was that he was being asked to do the impossible. At the heart of the contract, at the heart of the Business Link model, was the team of Personal Business Advisors (PBAs). Objective, well-informed, highly experienced business people, the PBAs were to be the core Business Link offer, working with businesses to diagnose and address their needs. They were to have the experience and insight of an industry leader, the listening skills of a Samaritan and a comprehensive, objective knowledge of all the specialist support on offer. And be willing to work for less than £30,000 per annum, if costs were to be kept within budget.

Tom tried and failed to find anyone to fit the spec. Eventually he settled for a team of recently redundant middle managers from banking and insurance, most of whom could be trusted to be both impartial and ineffective. This was an improvement on his first few recruits who proved to be self-serving and ineffective. With a new team, Tom's Business Link hit its customer engagement targets, gave isolated business owners someone to talk at, and did no great harm.

The civil servant contract managers were happy, government ministers felt they had done something useful that would win votes – and Tom tried to hide from the fact that the whole thing was off the point.

This is the **No Design for Manufacture** problem. Policy makers spot a problem they want to solve. They spend lots of time discussing how awful it is and command their paid officers to do something about it. But there is insufficient attention paid by policy makers and paid staff to what actually works. There is no point in doing something about a problem if what you do is irrelevant or makes the situation worse. Here are some examples.

- **Problem:** too many teenagers are getting pregnant.
  Solution: more sex education for young people.
  Result: Marginal.
  The point missed? Most young people know that pregnancy is caused by sex: their problem is not condoms but boredom. So we want to stop large numbers of young girls getting pregnant? Let's help them find meaning in their lives.

- **Problem:** People are driving too fast.
  Solution: Road traffic calming measures.
  The point missed? A false sense of safety leads to increased driving speeds and more accidents.

The **No Design for Manufacture** approach is endemic across the public sector. Processes introduced to ensure social workers achieve a consistent service in practice distract the individual from really listening to the client. Examples abound:

- Changes to nursing standards aimed at improving the quality of care mean the basics are neglected, hygiene standards fall, and infections go through the roof.
- The desire to make education more relevant and consistent leads

to repeated political tinkering with the curriculum, which leads to demotivated teachers – and teacher enthusiasm is one of the biggest determinants of successful learning.

I Command You To Innovate!

In 2002, central government invented the Regional Development Agencies (RDAs), one for each of the English regions. These new quangos were charged with drawing up an economic strategy for the region to which they belonged, and with using their regeneration funding as a catalyst for progressing the priorities contained within it.

Each RDA undertook extensive research and consultation. Each region produced impressive analyses of the economic characteristics and challenges of its area. The RDA set out priorities for public sector intervention and invested in the staff and organisational infrastructure to make things happen.

Not much changed. The RDAs' budgets, although in the hundreds of millions per annum, were too small to make much difference in their own right and struggled to provide much leverage over private sector investment or over the heavily centrally programmed public sector budgets spent on transport, social security, and health. The planned improvements in local competitiveness failed to materialise. The Regional Economic Strategies proved to have few points of connection with the people and assets which deliver economic competitiveness.

As one South Eastern entrepreneur said, **"You can write what plans you like, but it won't make a blind bit of difference to whether my business provides the products my customers want."**

Yet the existing orthodoxy still values planning above most other forms of activity. If the Regional Economic Strategies were failing, it could not be because the business of planning was the problem. It had to be the result of the plans being too limited in scope. So a new concept was invented in central government, the Integrated Regional Strategy, an even bigger strategy which would encompass not only the economic component but wider issues of land use, housing, and aspects of transport (previously included in another compendious and obstructive plan called the Regional Spatial Strategy). The belief was that, by achieving alignment between spatial and economic priorities, a region's political leadership could achieve significant positive leverage on competitiveness.

The Integrated Regional Strategies are currently in production. There is no reason to believe they will have any more efficacy than the Regional Economic Strategies. Indeed there is all of history (see Stalinist central planning as a start point) to suggest the complete reverse. They will probably be withdrawn before they are launched.

This is an example of the **Planning not Enterprise** challenge.

A public sector orthodoxy has developed which holds that action may not be taken until a full strategy and action plan is complete, preceded by extensive research.

In practice, the planning is often the only activity that happens: the actions planned never become real. The plain fact is that the most difficult public sector challenges are fluid, complex and not easily explicable; the kind of problems that do not respond well to plans; the sorts of issues that need an enterprising, not purely methodical, response.

Enterprise means trying things, learning, and changing.

The best way to solve the teenage pregnancy challenge, for instance, is to try a few things out on a small scale, see what works in a particular community and what does not, then stop what does not work and do more of what does. The best way to raise a region's competitiveness is not to have a tidy set of ordered priorities, since the future cannot be seen, especially by the state. The best way is to allow and encourage commercial mess, overlap and competition within the region, allowing the best to be tested and rise the top, ready to compete on a national and global stage. This is how Japan and Germany rose from the rubble of the Second World War.

Such an approach may need an infrastructure investment framework to put the basics in place – but not a comprehensive, consistent plan.

The desire for consistency is the enemy of innovation.

Again, these are not isolated examples of the problem. Almost every part of the public sector spends a huge proportion of its management time writing plans, vetting plans, monitoring performance against previous plans, or explaining why things have not turned out the way everyone expected. If plans were as powerful as they are ubiquitous, we would have no skills deficit (skills development plans), inter-community tension (community cohesion strategies), obesity (health promotion plans), and hate crime (hate crime strategies). We would have sustained economic success (competitiveness plans), high levels of well-being (child protection strategies), and an integrated transport system across the country (transport plans).

The fact that we do not have these things is due, at least in part, to an over-emphasis on planning and an under-emphasis on responsiveness and personal authority.

People As Work Units

Then there is our obsession with transactions, the **Transactions not relationships** problem. In attempting to be impartial, the public sector has learnt to be afraid of doing business based on relationships. *It has formally rejected the codes of trust, familiarity, and mutual* *advantage in favour of buying, measuring and managing transactions,* where transactions are things done – for instance, people trained, forms completed, cash handed over.

But what makes a difference on the ground, in the quality of service delivered, is often as much about the quality of relationships: the *care* provided, the *concern* expressed, the *long term familiar face.*

The transaction-not-relationship, doing but not connecting, management style is now so prevalent it goes unnoticed. If a nurse is managed according to actions completed, he is unlikely to go the extra mile in caring for his patients. If a teacher is judged according only to GCSE results, she is more likely to neglect the difficult student in favour of the potential high flyers, and will certainly have little incentive to encourage the development of the whole person through extra-curricular activities. If social work is managed according to the number of visits made to a family per week, the development of a relationship of trust between an individual social worker and the family will be ignored, and the possibility of a succession of different workers going in week after week becomes acceptable, demonstrating (from the family's point of view) *a level of state disrespect, which can do nothing to help their situation.*

So these three:

- **No design for manufacture**
- **Planning not enterprise**
- **Transactions not relationships**

are the basic problems with the way much of the public sector goes about its work, or is required to go about its work. An under-standing of these problems, what they look like, what causes them, what the alternatives might be, is fundamental to public sector troubleshooting.

Each of these three basic problem species appears in different guises. To be tackled, they first need to be identified, like threatening animals in the jungle. We will see how we can do this next.

PART TWO

NO DESIGN FOR MANUFACTURE

For the last few decades in the UK, the energy and directness of youth has been valued over the wisdom and compromise of age. This is true even in government, where intellect and energy are more important in policy circles than experience of what works. We have ended up electing politicians of increasing youth, advised by people of even greater inexperience from similar backgrounds, who then formulate policy on the basis of the way things ought to be.

Or we elect local councillors, not on the basis of their track record of successfully making things happen but, principally, on the basis of their having a combination of time and a bee in their bonnet about the way things ought to be.

But a lesson most of us have to learn the hard way is *that things are usually not the way they ought to be.* If you want to get something done, you need to look very hard at the way things actually are, and work with that. If you want to get people to go with you, you had better play close attention to what actually interests them, rather than what you think would be good for them.

This is the essence of enterprise, and it has particular relevance to the public sector. The **No Design for Manufacture** problems are, by definition, lacking in enterprise. There are seven of them.

1. Counter-Productive Design

In a car factory, product designers worked separately from the shop floor. Their ideas and their designs were brilliant, but often difficult, expensive or impossible to manufacture. The production line teams were blamed for the resulting poor product quality and reliability. Sales dropped. The company's survival was in doubt.

The production line teams sent a delegation to the Design Engineer's office.

"Why don't you design the cars in a way which is easy and cheap to build?" they said. "We could sell more cars, make more money and stay in business. They call this Design for Manufacture."

"Sorry," he said, "that's your problem. I'm employed to have ideas, not to make them real."

Public sector problems do not respond well to treatment. They feed off the wrong sort of solution and breed like rats. We give birth to more problems by handling our problems badly or by failing to change the approach as the problems evolve. We obsess about strategy without reference to the harsh realities on the ground.

For example, in the UK today, economic and social disadvantage has a close alignment with ethnicity. Or, to put it simply, you are much more likely to be poor, unemployed and under-qualified if you are not white. Apart from explicit discrimination, the primary causes are an inter-generational disadvantage (if your parents were unemployed, you are much more likely to be so) and inter-cultural clashes (if the way that you communicate with others is perceived, by the majority population, to be untrustworthy or aggressive, you are unlikely to succeed in mainstream markets).

Over recent decades, considerable local and national public funding has been spent addressing the problem. The white majority population has been taught, in the main, to find racial abuse offensive. Public cash has been spent on programmes and agencies aimed at the specific needs of specific minority ethnic groups. And progress has been made. There is less overt discrimination against minority ethnic groups. There are more Asian and African Caribbean people in senior positions in political, media, business, entertainment and sport. Some minority populations outstrip the averages in qualifications achievement and enterprise.

But at the general level, the problem remains: there is still a strong alignment between disadvantage and being non-white.

In some ways, the problem has worsened. As a result of the re-education of the public at large on unacceptable racial language, it has become difficult to talk about the issue at all, let alone what might be causing it. And there are signs of a growing resentment amongst poorer white people; a sense that all this attention and effort is being paid to the non-white disadvantaged population, because they are non-white, rather than because they are disadvantaged. Otherwise, the argument goes, why would that same attention not be given to all disadvantaged people, regardless of ethnicity?

As a consequence, the effect of some of this well-meaning public policy is to have created a greater awareness of race as a category, and greater mistrust of the public funding agencies. Grassroots organisations looking for public sector funding have found themselves adopting delineated positions, aligning with specific ethnic groups in order to meet funding conditions, competing with comparable organisations and their ethnic groups.

When an applicant fails to obtain funding, there is resentment: "How can you say my cause is not needy? Why have you funded that other ethnic group yet again?" Over time, the build-up of expectancy and resentment reinforces the gaps between groups.

The public sector originally addressed problems of disadvantage and ethnicity in a way which was well-intentioned and necessary. But as progress was made, greater subtlety was called for. Without this, the public sector's ethnic-specific intervention reinforced inter-ethnic tension. As a result, it potentially helps lock people into ethnic-specific ghettoes, blocks the enterprise which comes from diversity and contributes to social breakdown. It is in danger of worsening what it set out to solve.

The answer is to recognise that solutions must fit the way the world is, rather than the way it ought to be.

We have to create answers that can be implemented, rather than bright ideas that make complete logical sense but are fundamentally impractical or counter-productive. The acid test is whether people (agency staff, customers, communities, service users) will respond as planned. In this example, by addressing the issue as being primarily about the deprivation of specific ethnic groups, we may be attempting to break the inter-generational cycle, but we are reinforcing the divisions between ethnicities which helped create the problem in the first place.

The only real solution is to stop seeing the issue as an ethnic minority issue and see it instead as a deprivation issue. We must do something about disadvantage wherever it occurs, and ensure that the way we do it means that people from different ethnic backgrounds are encouraged (required) to work together. We must see the world, and the population, through 'disadvantage' spectacles, rather than ethnicity spectacles: we must invest in programmes that have a real effect on those areas of the country scarred by deprivation. The ethnic composition of those areas is relevant only to the extent that it helps shape our thinking on what will work.

Other examples of **Counter-Productive Design** are not hard to find:

- strategies to reduce the numbers on unemployment benefits which increase the take up of the more expensive disability benefit
- efficiency drives in Council Environmental Services, reducing winter gritting, which save small sums and result in a significant rise in the number of (hugely expensive and debilitating) broken wrists
- business support programmes which prop up failing businesses and obstruct the growth of their well-managed competitors
- police drug arrests that result in significant increases in crime levels as rival gangs fight over the newly available territory.

The heart of good troubleshooting strategy is to set out to do something which (1) improves things, (2) appeals to the customer, and (3) is possible.

2. Build an African Igloo

A European politician is asked to help with the problem of affordable housing in Africa. Too many people on the African continent are living in poor housing, suffering from the health and social ills which are the inevitable consequence. A solution is needed which is cheap and effective, requiring only local labour and materials to construct.

She looks around the world for examples of how this problem has been tackled successfully. Europe and America have little to offer her: their economic wealth is such that the average spend on an affordable housing unit is far in excess of what Africa could sustain. She eventually settles on the traditional Inuit Arctic housing solution: the igloo. It is technically straightforward, cheap to build and effective. Delighted with her research, she announces her solution to a meeting of African governments, securing a sizeable European overseas aid budget to support its implementation. After six months, she visits the programme to see how it is getting on. The project director greets her in an empty field.

"Where are the houses?" she asks.

"There are none," he replies. "We hit some problems."

"What problems?"

"First, there is no ice in Africa. But we solved that, although it was rather expensive, by building an ice plant locally. The second problem, which we are still working on, and I'm hopeful we will find a solution, is the strength of the African sun."

When you don't use a Design for Manufacture approach to public sector problems, you get an African Igloo: a simple, warm, well made, cheap to manufacture solution – built from an unavailable substance that anyway would melt before you got beyond the first layer of bricks.

The African Igloo approach *presupposes that interventions are transferable*. Igloos are an ideal solution in the Arctic: we have studied

22

how they are built in detail; we recognise that they are cheap to manufacture, provide high levels of insulation, are environmentally sustainable, and don't require high levels of specialist skills. We will therefore build them for the poor people of Africa.

The public sector is particularly prone to this disease.

- A politician sees a school working well in inner Glasgow and insists that it is the model for schools across the UK.
- A primary care trust adopts a particular approach in the South of England and the Department of Health requires that it is implemented across all health trusts.
- A vocational skills programme works well for hairdressing and is implemented for all other industries.

Much money is spent, much money is wasted, and a good number of people become frustrated and disillusioned. And the reason? Many successful solutions are simply not transferable. They are not transferable because the essence of the solution is not what is written down. The solution will be described and summarised – then that summary description treated **as if it were** the solution: *the account of the solution becomes the solution*. But the account is, of course, created by a person who may or may not be right in their analysis. And, however robust their analysis, their account cannot capture the *soul* of the approach. Typically, successful solutions to difficult public sector problems (and they are all difficult, because the easy ones have been solved) are down to:

1. charismatic leadership from the public sector side (not necessarily from the person who is the named programme leader)
2. active involvement from the service recipients
3. a large number of attempted (failed) solutions before the solution was found, resulting in a local desperation to make the next thing work.

So what is it we are transferring? A weak and partial description, rather than the rich texture of a shared endeavour grown from from the efforts, energy and shared history of a bunch of committed people. The igloo could work in Africa, but only if it was a house built of cow pats. And the Africans know how to build those, anyway.

So how do we avoid African Igloo solutions? Again, the answers are straightforward.

First, we must get the evaluations business right. Most public sector projects end up being 'evaluated'. We must ensure that, if we do evaluations, they are thorough and objective. If something has worked, let's celebrate. If it has not worked, let's celebrate that, too – at least we tried! – and identify, if we can, what we would have done differently (but watch out for the blame allocation). Evaluation is so often a box ticking exercise, playing to an empty house after the show has ended, when it ought to be seen as the most important item of all – since all public sector activity is temporary, yet public sector imperfections will always be with us.

Even more important than our attitude to evaluation, though, is *our attitude to transferability*; our tendency to assume, following a pseudo-scientific model, that a solution which works in one area will work in another.

We accept without question, for instance, that a programme to improve key stage 2 performance in one London school will work for all the schools in Wolverhampton. Leaving aside the question whether it is desirable to improve key stage 2 performance in isolation of achievement at other key stages, there are some important problems with such an assumption. The challenge is associated with the distinction between bounded and unbounded problems.

Bounded problems are those where all the variables can be known.

There may be many variables but they can, in principle, be listed. For bounded problems, an effective solution can be replicated, since the variables can be tracked and managed. So, the way you build a cruise liner in Britain will be directly relevant (transferable) to the way you build it in Singapore.

Unbounded problems have unknown variables: it is not possible to know all the relevant issues and factors. A riot can be described in fairly simple terms, but it cannot be predicted with complete accuracy, since a riot results from more causes than it is possible to know: the personalities of the people involved, their mood on the day in question, their experience of long term relative disadvantage, the layout of the street where it happened, international incidents, the temperature and weather and so on. The conditions for a riot are not, therefore, transferable: the police cannot say with 100% authority that a riot will occur on a specific date in a specific location. They can say only that, based on a set of known variables, a riot is more or less likely, not that it will happen. Similarly, an approach which successfully contained and suppressed a riot will not necessarily work well a second time, even though the situation appears similar.

In our work on the Lozells Disturbances of October 2005, for instance, we identified three ingredients necessary to that particular form of social unrest. *First*, you need a group or groups of people who perceive themselves to belong to a category (ethnic, age, gender, geographic location) which is subject to long term relative disadvantage. *Second*, you need, in this location, between identifiable groups, faultlines: a history of distance between people, based on their perceived identity. And *third*, you need some form of flash point which operates on that faultline. In Lozells, it was the alleged gang rape of a black girl by a group of Asian men.

This analysis has use: it demonstrates that long term effort is needed (to tackle disadvantage and the perception of disadvantage) as well as medium term relationship building (across faultlines), and short term containment (focusing on the flashpoint itself). *But it is not an analysis, nor is such an analysis possible, which can lead to a prediction of where future disturbances will happen.*

Nor is it possible to transfer the detailed responses to the Lozells disturbances across to any other communities with difficulties, other than in the most general terms. In truth, most of the best responses came from, and were particular to, the people who live in the area, working through, and leveraging, their network of relationships established over years, over generations.

For unbounded problems, we can learn from successful solutions to comparable problems. But we should use such models intelligently, interpreting them in the light of the issue we are faced with. With unbounded problems, if possible, it is best to try *more than one possible solution*, giving leadership to people who are close to the problem itself.

Progress should be robustly evaluated, with resources being taken from those approaches which have not proven themselves and transferred to those that are making progress. This is the only way to make progress in unpredictable circumstances – such as face most public sector areas.

We must also re-learn respect for *charismatic people*, for people who take action, for people who connect with people. We have become seduced by intellectual argument, by policy making in conference rooms and sitting rooms, by well-meaning but soft-handed progressives whose soul lies in the office not in the street. Some of our politicians have become such people, or have borrowed their clothes: *many have lost their human connection to the emotions of the people they represent.* Such people have an important place. But they are only one kind of people, and they do not have all the answers. With unbounded problems, no one has *all* the answers. Evidence-based policy making is useful, but not definitive.

Intuition and the ability to accept failure are as important as logic and the knowledge of what has worked elsewhere.

We must come to see public sector management as a *participation* sport. Good private sector service businesses learnt this a long time ago. If you are to be a successful retail manager, you have to be there with your staff and customers: you are, in your management role, an important part of the product – of the customer experience. Managers are not controllers, sitting in their control tower pulling levers. They are there on the shop floor, responding to issues that arise, steering the business and connecting with the customer.

Disadvantaged communities don't want regeneration done to them: they want people in authority to come and listen to their views – to show them respect. Job seekers don't (just) need jobs: they need self-respect, a sense of worth, the things that come from being listened to with humility and care. Then they may get to a place inside themselves where they are capable of keeping a job.

Architects who have been to Africa don't design igloos.

3. Make an Anti-Gravity Bike!

> A self-styled inventor sits down to design a new bike. He specifies a heavy frame, robust, hard wearing, resistant to damage. He sketches out wide wheels; stable, strong, capable of covering all terrains. He selects the best and most comfortable seat from an upmarket motorbike. And he realises that he has designed the perfect bike – except that it is too heavy for an ordinary person to pedal any distance. But this need not matter, since he decides to equip the bike with anti-gravity tyres. These have the effect of almost completely negating the weight of the bike overall, resulting in a piece of equipment which is both strong and efficient.
>
> The inventor takes his design to a manufacturer. "Make me this," he says. "It's a sure-fire success."
>
> The manufacturer looks at the designs. "We can do it," he says, after careful thought, "all except the tyres. There is no such thing as an anti-gravity tyre."
>
> "Fine," the inventor replies. "Just do the rest of the bike. I will advertise for someone else to supply the tyres."

The Anti-Gravity Bike is a close relative of the African Igloo. The African Igloo failed because an assumption was made about transferability: the igloo model did work, it just did not transfer from the Arctic to Africa. But the Anti-Gravity Bike never worked in any other environment than the designer's imagination. The Anti-Gravity Bike's design was based on how the designer thought the world might be, rather than on how the world really is. However sparkling the bike's frame, however powerful the brakes, however efficient the gears, if the bike relies on imaginary tyres it will not work.

The earlier Business Link story is an Anti-Gravity Bike example: the imagined Personal Business Advisors were the anti-gravity tyres.

Many of the worklessness strategies developed by local councils and their partners across the country are similarly flawed. Worklessness is the current public sector word to describe the problem of unemployment. Economic development officers observe that large new shopping centres, or major inward investors attracted to an area, can be successfully encouraged to take employees from the ranks of the unemployed. This is achieved by working with public money to design bespoke training courses, and by using job centre resource to coordinate between employer and unemployed candidate. If this use of public money – to coordinate and to deliver tailored training – works for large organisations, why not create such a mechanism for smaller businesses? Since the majority of new jobs will come from businesses at the smaller end of the scale, focusing on this market has to make sense.

It is true that smaller businesses are key to economic success and the growth of jobs. But the tailored jobs and training programme for small business is an Anti-Gravity Tyre solution; it's a fiction. Generally speaking, small businesses don't recruit the way big businesses do, setting out role specifications and seeking out the best candidate from the widest possible pool. Smaller businesses typically have a much less precise, more fluid sense of what they need; they are driven more by the need to find individuals they can work with and trust (since every recruit is such a major percentage of their workforce); they are often happiest to recruit through their existing social network (relatives, relatives of employees, professional contacts) since this reduces the chances of being taken for a ride. Small businesses see recruitment as a major risk; they recognise that it more about personality and alchemy than competence lists and science; they are not impressed by a **machine** solution (coordination and bespoke training) to a **personality** challenge.

The design mistake is usually the result of the designer (policy maker, or programme builder) knowing that *someone else, not the designer, will do the work* to make the design real. This is not because they are incompetent or mischievous: it is just a simple human truth – *things always look a good deal simpler to implement if it is someone else doing it*. A designer will always (often sub-consciously) gloss over or minimise the awkward bits if someone else is going to be the builder.

Those who do not fall for Anti-Gravity Bike mistakes are, in an important sense, enterprising. This is a further fundamental of the enterprising person: the ability to focus, in detail, on the grubby stuff which makes the difference between unproven bright idea and successfully implemented result. Anti-Gravity Bike solutions arise, again, from a general attachment to a pseudo-scientific approach. Management has come to be seen as a science. The world is awash with 'tools' and 'techniques' required for good management. Public sector managers, who do not have the simplicity afforded to their private sector cousins through the profit focus, are particularly vulnerable to the management science religion. In this religion, the priest (i.e. policy lead) sits in glorious isolation from the congregation (the people who actually have to make the policy work), with very little visceral sense of what is possible in the real world. He postulates solutions that, however well-meaning, are short on pragmatism.

Anti-Gravity Bike projects result in the same messes that characterise African Igloo solutions – only messier and more political, since they often result from the pet policy ideas of a leading figure who has built an organisation or political position around them. The alternative and more effective approaches are also similar:

- experiment with possible solutions
- build in customers' ownership from the start
- make it personal
- do more of what seems to work and less of what does not.

4. Throttle Our Suppliers!

> You are walking through a forest where you know there is a wolf. So you take your dog. You put him on a lead so that he will stay close to you and you hold him close because you are nervous. You hear noises behind the trees which make you more nervous, so you hold your dog on a shorter and shorter leash. In the end, you are holding him so tightly he cannot breathe. He dies. The wolf closes in.

This is a pretty close analogy of the way that public sector departments behave towards their quangos, or quangos behave towards their sub-contractors. Such is the fear that people will abuse the public purse, contracts are very closely specified and performance is tightly controlled through a large number of targets and intensive contract management. Over time, as new dangers are spotted, the contract specification and targets list grow in size, whilst the budget is reduced. The qualities of innovation and flexibility which were fundamental to why the agency or sub-contractor was created or appointed in the first place are stifled by degrees. In the end, the budget is too small to do even a basic job, the deliverer cuts one too many corners and is caught out or throws in the towel.

Examples are legion. Primary Care Trusts, Further Education Colleges, Regional Development Agencies, Grant Maintained Schools, Registered Social Landlords (housing associations) – all of these agencies were conceived as means to admit innovation and responsiveness into the system; all of them are incrementally reeled in by growing contract or inspection bureaucracy.

The now defunct Training and Enterprise Councils are a good case study. The TECs were set up in the 1990s by a Conservative government keen to enlist the drive and innovation of business people in increasing local enterprise and skills levels. 79 TECs were established across England as private limited companies, funded by central government, and charged with, amongst other things, commissioning job-specific skills training for unemployed young people and adults. Given considerable freedom in the early years, some TECs achieved great things, others were ineffectual.

Instead of closing the ineffectual players and handing their contracts to their well-run neighbours, government contract managers focused on tightening up the (centrally determined) TEC contract which dictated how the money could be spent, incrementally reducing the entrepreneurial latitude given to each TEC. At the same time, the 'unit price' paid for each successful outcome (for instance, a certified vocational training qualification achieved by a young person) was reduced. The vocational training providers, who acted as suppliers to the TECs, were forced to trim and trim again their delivery model.

In 1997 I left my role as head of a TEC, switching from gamekeeper to poacher, and taking a senior position in one of the largest national training providers. When I looked at what they provided I was shocked. *The TEC funds paid for no training at all.* The training provider's front line staff were simply form-filling assessors. They visited young 'apprentices' (in shops, offices or hairdressers), reviewed the extent to which they could show the range of competences required by the national standards for that professional at the relevant level (NVQ 1 to 4) and, where they fell short, told the employer that they needed to improve. The national training programme had been leached, in most vocational settings, to no more than an assessment process. There was still value in it, but pretty low value, and of questionable merit given the scale and cost of the organisational infrastructure that managed it. Much of the funding that passed through TECs was adding almost no value at all.

This pattern – of reducing budgets and increasing control over a five year cycle – is repeated throughout the public sector. The dog dies, there's a scary phase when no one knows what to do, then a new dog is found, a different lead is bought, and it starts all over again. And, very often, though the organisations have been restructured and renamed, the same individuals are doing pretty much the same jobs. The client sees very little change to a consistently poor service except for a twelve month downturn in support while the restructuring occurs every five years.

This situation arises from a fear of failure, the desire to avoid the abuse of public funds, and a *fear of the publicity associated with the abuse of public funds*.

It is rare, when a true Throttled Dog style is adopted, for there to be any negative headlines regarding businesses or organisations growing fat by abusing the public purse. Unfortunately, the Throttled Dog more than compensates for this success by consistently delivering failure and allowing for the systematic waste of public money – even though there is little attendant publicity to this effect. The delivery organisation spends most of its time servicing its contract interface. Time spent servicing its customer need plays a smaller and smaller part in its thinking. So specific do the contractual requirements become that the delivery partner has no option but to orientate their business as if the funder were the customer, treating the real customer (the public) as if they were so many heads of cattle; mere numbers to enable the delivery of targets.

As the budgets reduce, the discretionary elements of delivery are removed, stripping the service back only to those parts that are contractual requirements (which tend to be those that add least value). Eventually, inevitably, corners are cut, even the essentials are not delivered, but targets continue to be met and ministers are happy to boast about the results achieved. But the customer has a second rate, impersonal or irrelevant service. This must surely qualify as abuse of public funds. And the fact is that *this goes on all the time across the public sector*.

It happens not through incompetence but through fear: fear of the media exposing salacious details concerning the waste of tax payers' money; fear that the delivery agency will not do what the people at the centre consider to be obviously good practice. The dog is held on a short leash and is throttled. If it were let off the leash, it would have the chance to prove itself. And if, occasionally, it proved to be ineffective, or dishonest (running with the wolves), we would be no worse off than we were – but at least we would have given ourselves a chance of success.

In short, the solution lies in the *proper management of risk*. If we recognise that the very short leash represents a big risk (that is, a high chance of failure), then it becomes easier to take the lesser risk of allowing the delivery agency more scope and flexibility. If we recognise that too many targets actually inhibit an organisation's ability to perform, we will be more likely to constrain the number of targets we impose. This approach also requires that we pay close attention to the quality of the delivery agency. Where the leash is short, and the funder is in control, an uninspiring delivery agent is unlikely to be binned, even though the customer is getting poor service – since the effort required to bin them is considerable, and there is more likelihood of bad publicity.

But where the delivery agency has a longer leash and more discretion, it is critical that the funder is robust in its contract management and in its requirement for *customer-focused performance success*.

5. The "Bleeding Stumps" Argument

Beggar:	Look how unfortunate I am!
Observer:	How can you get better?
Beggar:	Why would I want to get better?
Observer:	If you are better, you can work and have a good life.
Beggar:	But look at my bleeding stumps! The more revolting I look, the more money I make.

Disproportionately large amounts of public sector management time are taken up with money: where to get it; how to spend it. One funding game is particularly self-defeating. In this game, central government invites its agencies (local government, quangos, or suppliers) to compete for the available pot of funds for a specific purpose. Only a limited number of bidders are funded. The remainder take the blame. And government gets to allocate a smaller than ideal budget to whatever the issue is, in the knowledge that someone else will be seen to be at fault.

In order to win the money, the agency has to prove that the needs of the client group are greater than the needs of its competitors. It has to demonstrate *severity of need* and show how wonderful are its plans to do something about it.

As a result, all bidding organisations get themselves worked up into a lather about the problems of their client group. When an applicant organisation succeeds in obtaining funding, having had to amass information about the dire circumstances which warranted it, the resultant emotion is not gratitude but expectancy – "We had a right to this" – combined with irritation at the inevitable accompanying bureaucracy. When an applicant fails to obtain funding, there is resentment – "How can you say my cause is not needy? Why have you funded that other group yet again?"

I have worked with a number of deprived urban areas which have been the recipients of a series of such funds from central government, most recently from the Single Regeneration Budget, New Deal for Communities and others, like Housing Market Renewal. These are areas with genuine challenges: high levels of unemployment and disadvantage, low skills levels, emerging gang problems and some very poor quality housing. They may also be highly diverse, vibrant and occasionally tense. If there is help to be had, such places deserve to be in the running for it.

But these areas do not need just any help – they need good, consistent help. What they have seen is big promises at the start of a new programme, followed by squabbles over programme governance, followed by an inability to prioritise and plan, followed by a rush to spend before the money goes, with the spend bouncing back off the local economy into the pockets of the middle class, followed by the programme closing earlier than anticipated as political attention wanders elsewhere. There may then be a couple of years of neglect, before another bright idea is launched as – "This time it will be different!" – new promises are made. And every time this happens local people are told again just how needy they are.

Unintentionally, the public sector sets itself up as the Parent, and tells local people they are the Child; *dependency is reinforced, local asset values are undermined; the poorest are further de-capitalised.*

Whether successful or not, all public sector organisations become accustomed to defining themselves by the neediness of their client base, rather than their strengths and the path towards independence. If you are striving for client improvement, this is not the optimum outlook to adopt.

Both central government and the bidding agencies are at fault. Central funds should not be allocated on the basis of this form of competition. Funds should follow an objective assessment of need. There may be useful competition concerning how the funds should be used within an area, because this encourages delivery innovation and flexibility. But whether the funds should be allocated in the first place? It is not appropriate for this judgement to be politically sidestepped in this way.

The bidders are in a difficult position: it is hard not to be seduced into competing. None the less, too infrequently do potential bidders stand up and say, "No, not on those terms, we have our pride." But if they must bid, the agencies should work harder to ensure that the Bleeding Stumps narrative is kept to the confines of the bid: that it is not allowed to seep out and shape the self-image and aspirations of the target population.

I have been closely associated with the latest programme and organisation in one particular inner-city area. As I write we are focusing our efforts on looking through the other end of the telescope: seeing how the funds can be used to recapitalise the poor, to create an organisation which is genuinely rooted and accountable locally, with a sustainability which lasts a generation, with a focus on supporting local enterprise and pride. The basics of how to do this – *good governance, local asset ownership, community development techniques, proper communication and accountability* – are well understood, but rarely practised.

6. Charge of the Light Brigade

> The Charge of the Light Brigade was a disastrous cavalry charge led by Lord Cardigan during the Battle of Balaclava on 25 October 1854 in the Crimean War. It was an impressive action, and extremely costly; but misdirected and irrelevant to the progress of the battle.
>
> French Marshal Pierre Bosquet observed:
>
> *"It is magnificent, but it is not war. It is madness."*

When a problem occurs, politicians (local or national) are particularly keen on taking impressive action. Decisiveness in a crisis is, of course, a necessary attribute of leadership. But too often, the 'impressive' action taken is futile, expensive – and counter-productive.

For example, a government's scrapping of low end stamp duty will not prop up the housing market. It will not even win a government any more votes, since, when the tinkering fails to have an impact, it simply makes the action look weak. The sacking of a quango's Chief Executive may satisfy the politician's need to be seen to act when there has been a problem, but will not help the organisation address the immediate crisis.

The public sector's addiction to such action; the managerial and budgetary attention it takes; these things distract from the true task, which is to ensure the problem is contained before it happens. Real solutions usually start at least five years before the crisis. Which is another way of saying that, right now, the public sector must start laying the foundations for solutions which will remove future crises – from global warming to a Chinese arms race to a fatal epidemic.

Early action will never be popular because, by definition, the wider majority of people will not see the need. But is this not why we have leaders? Would it not have been better for the government to have stood up to the City and contained its excesses well before the banking crisis? For the Prime Minister of the day to have looked foolishly risk-averse? Even for that Prime Minister subsequently to have been voted out of office as a result, and then to have looked wise indeed when the American banks collapsed – than to have let the inevitable crisis happen as it did?

For this to happen *we need our politicians to know that we will respect and vote on the basis of their principles and courage*; that the population will accept the need for leaders to take difficult decisions, even to the extent of invading another country, if the processes that led to that decision have been as thorough as time allows, and the decision has been based on sound moral considerations.

7. Follow the Guidance!

Lazy Game Play

John G was the Chief Executive of a sizeable quango. He would say in private that he had no interest in the mission of the organisation. He saw his job as, very simply, to closely examine his annual government contract and work out how he could, with the least effort, hit the targets specified within it – regardless of whether, in so doing, he had any positive effect on the intended recipients of his service.

John G's organisation came high up in the league tables for comparable quangos – which used, of course, the government-allocated activity targets as the basis of its rankings. The geographic area for which he was responsible, on the other hand, continued to rank at the bottom end of the population index for the underlying issue he was there to address.

In the private sector, someone who does a great job has a reasonable chance of being rewarded. The common currency of the private sector (return on investment) means that good work can often be reasonably connected with increased profit, which can reasonably easily result in personal reward.

In the public sector, doing a great job is not enough. There are usually targets and measurables, but they are often more a statement of minimum requirements, rarely being capable of capturing the essence of exceptional performance. Sometimes the targets actually seem to get in the way of great service.

It is important to recognise the political realities here. No one has a chance of being recognised for exceptional public sector performance unless they have also ticked the box for target achievement. John G's approach was not entirely wrong. He recognised the fact that he could do nothing unless he was being *seen* to perform. In the absence of hitting his targets, however arbitrary they were, he would not have the budget and the freedom to do things that mattered.

Where he fell short was: (1) in not being interested in delivering the targets in ways which also added value to the customer; and (2) in not caring about developing additional, innovative solutions to the problems of his population by using the margin he could earn through efficiently achieving his targets.

Hospital waiting list targets can be hit by redefining an early consultant consultation as being an admission; or they can be achieved by making the overall system more efficient, aligning supply more effectively with demand and using savings achieved to invest in a health promotion campaign to change the behaviours which are the principal cause of the disease.

The John G example is important. The plain, unpalatable fact is that public sector organisations must deliver on the imposed targets/measurables (waiting lists, NVQs, new builds, etc) if they are to stand a chance of adding value in the additional ways they consider important. They can, of course, separately lobby for a change to the targets – but that is a longer term game; a different game.

PART THREE

PLANNING NOT ENTERPRISE

There is a pattern in the way civilisations progress. Societies live with an issue for a while, whether it be disease, sanitation, spiritual angst or any number of other challenges to the human condition en masse. Then an imaginative thinker finds a solution. The solution is at first rejected, then copied by the few, then standardised and rolled out to the many. It then becomes normal, assumed: a right. A management edifice is built on it; it is tweaked, tuned and improved to suit every nuance of taste; the basic principles become neglected under the weight of process manuals and management committees; the system decays and the problem returns. This is the life cycle of a religion, a health system, even transport. *Their youth is enterprise, their middle age is standardisation, their decline is bureaucracy.*

Trapped in an Orthodoxy

Because we are surrounded by solutions generated two or more generations ago, we see bureaucracy as the norm. We believe that structured planning is the way to address new socio-economic ills. *We forget that solutions start with enterprise, not with planning.*

Any amount of central planning will have only limited effect in trying to get greater alignment between health services for old people paid for by PCTs and delivered by GPs or hospitals, and care services for old people paid for by Councils and delivered by private and third sector businesses. Rather than asking the managers, who have much to lose from any change, to produce ever more complex plans, the best results may be achieved by taking a more radical approach called *personalisation*. In this model, the budget for certain categories of treatment is transferred to the client, who then decides how it should be spent. Done well, change sweeps rapidly through the system, in line with need. Personalisation is not achieved with no plans at all, but the plans can be much leaner, much more real. They are plans to introduce flexibility into the system. The system can then develop in ways that could not be predicted.

For decades, central government has grappled with the problem of local government: the poor quality of many councils and councillors, the waste and inertia of locally managed public services. A great weight of planning, targets, audits, performance management regimes and guidance has been generated to deal with the issue – improving performance to a degree, yes, but being accompanied by a continued hollowing out of local democracy, a sense of political disempowerment amongst the population at large (what does it matter if I do or do not vote in local elections, since few real decisions are made locally?), and huge administrative overheads.

Making Politics Matter

An alternative approach – counter-intuitive but effective – is easily achieved. *Were central government to pass substantial budgets and decision making back to local government, local politics would start to matter again.*

Local people would elect better quality politicians, better local decisions would be made, and the overpowering central performance management regime could be dispensed with. In the short term there would be considerable pain and central government would have to be ready to step in when lunatic regimes were messing things up – but the overall results would be a significantly more effective and efficient solution than we have at present. This is, after all, what democracy is all about: flawed, imperfect, in need of the continued attention and involvement of those who care – but better than the alternatives.

8. This Is A Pipe!

This is not...

The painter Réné Magritte's (1898-1967) work, *Ceçi n'est pas une pipe* ("This is not a pipe") calls into question the process of visual representation itself, since what is painted on canvas is not actually a pipe, but a depiction of a pipe. The picture's title, which is part of the artwork, draws attention to the fact that there is no equivalency between a pipe and the image of a pipe. A similar concept is contained in the phrase, "the map is not the terrain".

The public sector is good at producing and commissioning documents. The documents talk in terms of imperatives, resources and actions. But no document has any worth – it can indeed be worse than worthless – unless it results in positive change, unless it results in action. And an action *statement* is not an action, just as a picture of a pipe is not a pipe.

When I was asked to write the report into the Lozells Disturbances of 2005, I was not keen. What was asked for was a document setting out why the near-riots had happened and what should be done about it. It was very clear that there are as many different truths about the chaos which happened on those few days in October as there were people involved or affected. I was conscious that an inevitably selective narrative about the causes would be forced to use a generalising vocabulary ('young men', 'the Police', 'the Asian community') which could all too easily reinforce those unwarranted stereotypes which lead to generalist and impersonal public sector 'interventions' which would simply reinforce the sense of marginalisation which underpinned much of the tension. When I accepted the commission I did so on the understanding that I would write something which would set out to have **utility** only; which would not try to be definitive; which would only – but importantly – help the public sector take a step forward in reducing the likelihood of it happening again. Early on, the document notes:

The report should be read with caution. It is not, and cannot be, comprehensive. There are no easy or tidy answers to a problem which, at an underlying level, has existed in and around Lozells for generations. Our central contention, that the strengthening of relationships of all sorts is the only real and long term solution, is not greatly advanced by the writing or reading of a report. Relationships are personal, not institutional. They require real investment – and risk – from all individuals who think that the issue is important.

And it concludes as follows:

Since the riots of the 1980s, the processes and mechanisms which the public sector has set up to address health, housing, employment, skills, regeneration and social needs are still there in one shape or form, still employing the people (mostly not from Lozells) who work in them. Yet the health, housing, employment, skills, regeneration and social problems remain. It is no surprise, therefore, that the average Lozells citizen might see little value in such mechanisms, over and above the slim employment opportunity the agencies themselves represent; that the average citizen might feel that the system does not care.

Systems, of course, cannot care. People can. The challenge is to design the systems so that they are able – even required – to do so.

The cynical view is that working on these documents – and documents do tend to dominate the sector – is a seductive alternative to doing things that will actually make a difference. The average person in the street is at a complete loss to account for what public servants do all day, in their meetings, with their documents, emails and BlackBerrys.

The charge is that that the reports' strategies are irrelevant. This is often true. There are some compelling responses to this charge: that it is only by extensive discussion, leading up to the development of a strategy document or plan, that the various parties which need to be involved can come to agreement; that the strategy process flushes out the key priorities, ensuring that resources are allocated accordingly, rather than as they have always been; that the strategy is necessary for public sector accountability and probity in providing a reference point against which progress can be evaluated.

These are compelling responses. Unfortunately, they are very rarely seen through in practice. The plain fact is that *too much time is spent on forming words on paper, and too little time is spent on taking action.* Such is the value the public sector places on the ability to express itself with clarity and precision that wordy people get promoted more quickly than action people. So action people either learn to become wordy people, get disillusioned and become ineffective, or get disillusioned and leave. As a result, *the public sector is significantly less action-oriented and effective than, given its size, resources and brain power, it should be.*

What is the answer?

- We need the wordy people to see the light and become more action-oriented.
- We need meetings, all meetings, to focus on what actions are to be completed, and to ensure that the previously agreed actions are seen through.
- We need to keep planning and strategy focused, rapid and quantitative in style.
- We need to focus on resolving areas of disagreement, rather than on finding words that dress disagreement up as alignment.
- We need to allow passion and energy back into the room.
- Where we use external resources (consultants), we need to use

them to facilitate agreement and to take action, not (just) to write documents.

We need, in short, a culture change. This needs to be led by all of us (but it does not need a big culture change project or strategy!) From the **top**, the *politicians and senior managers must ask not for frameworks, strategies and checklists – but focus points and priority actions.* From the **bottom**, the *people in the front line must invite senior people to come and see, rather than send them a report.* And the **middle**, *managers must make contact with the customer/service user a key component of how they assess progress.*

Strategy – good or bad – is actually a number of different things. We will come back to this later.

And what of the Lozells report? In the couple of years immediately after the disturbances, it made, I think, very little difference. What progress there was in the area was led by committed local people making things happen. The public sector supertanker carried on its way. But, more recently, I do think a positive change can be identified which is at least in part a consequence of the report's recommendations. This dealt with attitude: *the need for public service providers to see their relationship with local people as just that – a relationship – rather than seeing people as the passive recipients of centrally designed interventions.* A genuine commitment to this approach has slowly led to a significant change in service culture.

The report was not the culture change, and can not even be said to have caused the culture change; but it was probably useful in helping it on its way.

9. Start with the Sledgehammer!

> How can we really understand and appreciate the Taj Mahal?
>
> One way of doing so is to take sledgehammer to it: to break it down into pieces, to measure and catalogue each piece, to model the relationship between each piece and each other piece. At the end of such an exercise you would have a very detailed and complex model of the building and a thorough analysis of the materials which made it up. But you would have destroyed the building.

There is a large number of good brains working in the public sector. Many, without explicitly recognising it, have been trained in a particular way of thinking; the *analytical-sequential mode*. This is essentially an approach which breaks down an issue into its component parts, generates possible solutions, identifies the optimum solution set, plans how the solution will be implemented, then acts. The method is logical, seductively intellectual, and occasionally effective. The approach, which tends to use an engineering or systems vocabulary, has become part of a pseudo-scientific orthodoxy across many walks of life, and the public sector is no more immune than society in general. 'Evidence-based policy' is an example of this way of thinking. But it is just one approach, not *the* approach.

The Analytical Sledgehammer approach has the following characteristics:

- It refuses to see a problem as part of a wider set of issues.
- It addresses symptoms, not causes.
- It perpetuates the people-as-atoms philosophy which undermines the fabric of our communities.
- It seeks to avoid risk rather than to manage it.
- It places the analyser outside the problem, allowing (requiring) emotions to be stripped out of the thinking.

- It assumes there is a right answer which, if only it can be revealed, can be delivered – rather than recognising that the best we can have is progress in the right direction, since there are *often no right answers*.

Take gang violence. The Analytical Sledgehammer sees it only as a crime and disorder issue. It refuses to make the obvious links to school exclusions (resulting in both disaffection and the time to cause trouble) and to young male fundamentals (the testosterone-driven need to test the authority of the dominant male). It blames parents. It looks to contain or cure the perpetrators, even though the "support" of authority is precisely what they are reacting against. It does not take into account that the violence of young men has been in our society for a very long time; that it was the force which, channelled, for good or ill, built empires and won wars.

Take hospital infections, including MRSA. The Analytical Sledgehammer sees it as a sign of poor nursing standards or poor hospital management. It does not see the link with the requirement to reduce waiting lists (resulting in greater hospital over-crowding); to bureaucracy (more form filling means less disinfecting); and to outsourcing of menial functions (which fragments responsibility for cleanliness). It looks to cure the problem with further checklists and frameworks for managers and nurses to complete – who checks these forms other than in the aftermath of an adverse event, in order to absolve themselves of blame? – rather than by recognising that hygiene will always be an issue in hospitals (warm places full of sick people) and that the best solution is to give well trained people the responsibility and time they crave to make it better.

The approach sees a person as a service user, supplier, public sector worker or voter – but it is not capable of seeing a person as potentially all four: as a *person*. As a consequence, the life goes out of the solutions generated. Employees are treated as if they were simply programmable instruction takers in the belief that, if only there were a long enough checklist or a sufficiently detailed framework, there would be no more issues. Customers are treated as passive, needing support, rather than as active agents whose sense of their own involvement – and responsibility – is a major factor in their ability and willingness to move on.

And, since risk is screwed out of the system, there is no room for innovation. We are constantly surprised by new problems which don't fit the old frameworks, and continually looking to allocate blame when the checklists are not followed because they have become unwieldy.

Finally, by treating our target people as if they were entirely defined as members of the group in question – for instance, members of a gang, or a hospitalised elderly person – we are in danger of standardising our services in line with a set of assumed characteristics which go with that group even though the individual may not conform to the stereotype, and potentially reinforcing the very problem we are trying to solve. If the system tells a gang member that he is violent, he may become so. If the system tells an elderly hospital patient that he can do little for himself, this may become true.

The Analytical Sledgehammer is the default approach used across the public sector, often – and this is the terrifying bit – without knowing that it is being used: without knowing that there is another way. The reasons are straightforward. We live in a systems age: we are all trained, formally and informally, to think systematically – or to think that we ought to.

Politicians, ever anxious to demonstrate how leading edge they are, and how business-like, have fallen in love with the private sector notion of targets. Few areas of public service are not now driven by targets. And targets do have (or can have – see later) utility in the public sector, but they have to be used with care. One of the common ways they are misused matches directly with the Analytical Sledgehammer philosophy. The error goes like this: if there is a target, there must be an activity directly aligned with that target. If we are trying to reduce drug abuse amongst teenagers, we need a drug abuse reduction programme for teenagers. Such seductive logic ignores the fact that the best way to reduce teenage drug abuse might be to improve leisure facilities or introduce a new sports tournament – or generally do a wide range of things other than run adverts which, due to the contrary nature of the teenage mind, easily become seen as promoting a grunge-chic image of drug taking.

So the fundamental solution is one of mindset. Everybody in the public sector, from politicians and policy makers through to on the ground implementers, should recognise that there are alternative ways of coming at problems than the Analytical Sledgehammer approach. A problem can approached in a number of ways, including these.

- **As an holistic system**
  If it must be seen as an engineering problem (this causes that, so let's address this), it should at least be seen as a **complete** engineering problem. So, not all the causes of a crime and disorder problem are themselves crime and disorder issues; not all health problems can be solved through health interventions; low skills levels may result from low self-esteem as well as poor training.

- **As a relationship network**
  A person can be seen as the recipient of a particular public service – or as a person and a node in a web of relationships. Taking this last view, we might reframe our problem in ways which suggest quite different solutions approaches. As a social landlord, concerned at significant rent arrears in a particular area, we might look for connections between problem tenants; we might look for patterns of relationships between them and our own staff,

between them and the staff of other agencies, between them and other dynamics (for instance, employment) in their overall environment. As a result, solutions other than more aggressive rent collection may suggest themselves: peer pressure, for instance; or mutual self-help.

- **As a risk balance**
  If we accept that risk cannot be excluded or avoided, *we have to accept risk in our solutions.* When once we accept this, a wider range of alternative solutions become possible, over and above the risk-minimising approach which is standard. The risk minimising approach usually involves creating a problem-specific programme or intervention, setting targets, hitting those targets, then acknowledging that – for "unforeseeable reasons" – the targets did not make much difference to the underlying problem. In other words, *the risk minimising solution actually carries the greatest risk of all* – that we allow the problem to go unchecked but think we are doing something about it. The best solutions to gang problems often happen when we work with and through the gang leaders. These are, after all, often young men with considerable leadership and entrepreneurial skills who, on reaching their early/mid-twenties, tend to develop a more adult sensibility, recognising their responsibility to their younger charges and becoming keen to explore positive ways forward. But the 'system' can find it hard to countenance public servants working with, even funding, known offenders.

- **As a blame balance**
  This perspective follows on from the risk balance outlook. *We must accept that the public sector will always be characterised by blame,* by people blaming and people seeking to avoid blame. This is an inevitable consequence of how we do politics in the UK, and the growth of consumerism. If we recognise that blame is part of the milieu, and look at the problem from a blame perspective

(Who gets blamed? How much blame? When will the blame surface? How much blame happens if we don't act?), again, a whole range of new solutions may become available to us. We might know, for instance, that there are no automatic answers to a housing estate's anti-social behaviour problems; that the only viable solution is to try a range of solutions to see which work; and that there will therefore inevitably be projects or activities which fail. And we might believe that the antagonistic local press will pick up on any such failures as further evidence of our own organisation's public sector inefficiency. In this situation, the smart thing to do at the outset is to *identify which players can, with impunity, or even with credit, take the blame* should the issue arise, and to position them to take the blame in the most effective way possible. An organisation's private sector non-executive board member, for instance, may be very happy to stand up and take responsibility for what is essentially an entrepreneurial approach: she may well be prepared to meet with the local press and draw the sting of the issue before the programme starts – after all, being a risk-taker is part of her self-image and may suit her own corporate profile building.

- **As insoluble**

  If we are grown up about this, and recognise that many public sector problems never go away, then we will stop having to pretend that we are building complete and final answers. We can instead focus on building what is possible – *solutions that make progress*. The Northern Ireland Peace Process worked because, whatever people felt about their differences, when once they had tasted a period without violence they would not allow their leaders to go back to the gun. Though the sides could not agree an end point, they could keep the peace by making progress in the direction of cooperation.

Similarly, though the poor are always with us, we can work to ensure that no-one individual is doomed to be poor from the moment of their birth. If we recognise that a problem is fundamentally insoluble, we are then liberated to think through how we can contain it or reduce it. Britain's drug strategy, for instance, has manifestly failed. It is clear that a punitive approach to drug taking, which attempts to squeeze drugs out of the national system, has not succeeded in reducing harmful drug use. Quite the reverse, it has driven up the street value of drugs, making the industry more attractive to new entrants, and driving addicted users to crime and prostitution. And it means that a customer can never be sure of the quality of what he is buying. An alternative approach would be to legitimise all drug use, allowing drug manufacture (under quality controlled conditions), significantly reducing prices and crime; and allowing the public sector spend to shift from the criminal justice system (police, customs) to health (addiction prevention and care).

- **Intuitively**

In the UK public sector we tend to avoid using words like 'intuition'. It smacks of half-baked impulsiveness, the worst kind of American TV detective series; a lack of conformance to established good practice. Yet it is interesting how often, especially for experienced players, *intuition about why something happened, about how to address a problem, can be more effective than logic.*

The reason is simple and not in the least fluffy. The human brain has an enormous capacity for memory and for the identification of patterns. When we see a problem, we may not consciously call up comparable problems from our past, but our sub-conscious will be busy working out the essential pattern of variables, identifying comparable occurrences, and cross-referencing to likely future out turns. Our intuition can be pretty good at spotting what to do – if we are able to hear it. An experienced local authority Chief Executive or senior officer ought to have a feeling for the right way to solve a problem; her political masters ought to expect her to do so; and neither should automatically seek external consultants (especially if they are less experienced than the woman herself) to come up with a better answer. For a wide range of challenges, *it is often the case that doing something quickly and with conviction is more effective than taking time to think through the "best" way forward.*

A confident and high profile response to a riot, to a growth in gang violence, to hospital infection control problems, to a downturn in the local economy, to poor school exam results – a decisive response can create a positive momentum which can then be flexed as clearer ideas on best practice become available. A slow and considered response, though appropriate for some issues, can lead to inertia, passivity, and in-fighting.

This is not a plea for lazy thinking. The sequential-analytical approach is a fundamentally important tool in the public sector and should not be neglected. But it has shortcomings. Effective solutions happen when the problem has been properly understood. And understanding the problem happens when *it is examined from a range of different perspectives*, through a range of different prisms. There are those who understand the world by watching it, from a distance, through a telescope while making detailed notes. There are those who understand the world by diving in and swimming with the dolphins.

Same world, different understandings, both valid.

10. Add More Targets!

Many of us are overweight and suffer for it, in terms of self-esteem, health, energy levels, perceived attractiveness to potential partners, and length of life. We diet, to try to lose that weight. The diet may work in the short term, but before long the weight goes back on. The diet reduces the weight but often does not address the fundamental behaviours and attitudes which caused the weight gain in the first place. If you are in the business of supplying products and services to dieting people, you have a population of customers desperate for your next innovation, a population which only ever increases in size. Dieting is a good business to be in.

Dieting can work, of course, but only if the person on the diet does not focus on the diet to the exclusion of the rest of their lifestyle; their exercise levels, their outlook, their relationships. Crash diets are the worst of all. Dieting works if it is part of a long term change in lifestyle and attitude.

Targets are like diets. They can have the opposite effect to that intended. We have noted that targets are not the same as results. Having an idea of how you would like the world to be does not equate to knowing what you are going to do to achieve it. Targets are usually created by the funder, contract writer, policy maker or programme designer, sometimes by reference to the better state of affairs as measured elsewhere or in the past, sometimes by reference to what might be imagined to be a favourable future. Either way – whether they are grounded in some sort of reality or not – the target giver can impose unrealistic and over-directive pressure on the target implementer. If the contract manager has too clear an idea of the measurements and targets, it will likely be counter-productive, since it will require the deliverer to focus on the proxy issue (the target) at the expense of the reason why the work is being done.

If it has been decided, for instance, that we need to reduce the level of hate crime (racism, homophobia, Islamophobia etc), it is all too easy for the person or organisation charged with doing so to launch an anti-hate crime programme. This might comprise, for instance, a crack down on known offenders, briefing sessions in schools and improvements in city centre closed-circuit television. Yet the fundamental causes of hate crime might be associated with much more deep rooted issues, concerning how people are segregated, or self-segregate, into homogenous groups across different parts of an urban area; it might be to do with new waves of immigration being concentrated in already crowded, poor areas, or with flaws in the housing allocation process; it might be a result of basic value system clashes, and a misinterpretation by one group of the degree of respect another group is displaying towards them. Though the crime and disorder initiatives are worth doing, it is by working with these more difficult issues that we will make sustainable, deep rooted progress.

But the target mentality, by implying that every target needs an action which is couched in exactly the same terms and which addresses the target head on (in a crash diet manner), can obstruct these longer term solutions. Sometimes a crash diet is necessary to save a person's life. Similarly, sometimes hard targets and fixed timescales are necessary. But, *unless they are accompanied by support for longer term, more fundamental change, they won't stick – and may worsen the situation.*

Targets also rely on measurement. There is little point in setting a target unless there is a measurement mechanism which enables progress tracking, or the target setter has the resources to create one. This is surprisingly often forgotten: so many times we see progress reports with boxes containing some variant on the statement "not yet measured" – as if this were an acceptable position to be in. And sometimes both sides behave as if, just by having set targets, they have done what needs to be done. Performance against targets is either not reported, or a lack of performance (the result of having done nothing different since the targets arrived) is explained away:

1. "We never did think this was a good target"
2. "The way they are measuring it is irrelevant to our circumstances"
3. "Well, I could hit this target if you are that worried about it, but it would obviously mean that I would have to direct resources away from this other thing you care about".

And targets can lead to unintended behaviours of another, more problematic kind. Hate crime again provides a good example of this. Part of the problem with hate crime is under-reporting: minority groups (for instance, gay people, people from specific ethnic minority communities) may find it hard to trust the system to take their complaint seriously, and will often not report a hate crime. Effective hate crime strategies therefore look for an increase in the percentage of offences that are reported – which means, in the short term, an increase in the absolute number of reported hate crimes in an area. The strategy would also seek to reduce, inevitably over a longer period, the number of hate offences committed in the first place. Inevitably, the delivery agencies are asked to take on two conflicting targets: (1) more reporting of hate crimes (measured by the number of hate crimes reported relative to the previous year); and (2) a reduction in hate crime (measured by the number of hate crimes reported). In this situation, the people leading on delivery are almost bound to take a pragmatic view, recognise that their political masters will, when it comes to performance assessment, be looking for evidence of a reduction in crime, and therefore put a priority on managing down reported crime levels. Their work on increasing people's willingness to report the crime will be at best half-hearted.

Targets can be achieved in ways which have very little to do with fundamental change, and a great deal more to do with self-protection. If we set targets, we look for performance in terms of progress against those targets – quite reasonably. And if we judge performance in those terms, we judge an **individual's** performance accordingly. And if you know that you, as an individual, will be judged according to specific targets, you look for ways of ensuring those targets are hit. Most people will look for legitimate ways of demonstrating performance, but they will not be too worried if their approaches conform to the letter, rather than the spirit, of the performance framework. Neither will their bosses, since their bosses will be judged on the same basis.

To return to hate crime: what we want is a reduction in hate crime levels. If we measure this (very reasonable) desire in terms of the numbers of convictions, we put pressure on all points of the system (police, crown prosecution service etc) to reduce the number of cases going to court, not the number of assaults. So that would not be a good way of measuring. If we measure it in terms of the number of reported hate crimes, we are in effect putting pressure on the system not to log crime reports as being instances of hate crime, or to try to discourage a victim from reporting at all.

In fact, what we need, to reduce hate crime levels, is an increase in the extent to which the population at large find hate crime unacceptable, increasing social pressure on potential offenders not to do it, which would result, in the short/medium term, in *more* hate crime victims coming forward to the police. A better target might therefore be an **increase** in hate crime reporting. But, to avoid the danger that this might result in even more aberrant behaviour, we might back this up by creating a separate measurement mechanism, based on the British Crime Survey approach, which independently measures people's experience of (particular categories of) crime.

This is not to say that we don't need targets: we do. Overweight people need to be on an appropriate diet. But targets, like diets, need to be handled carefully, as part of a bigger management programme. The rules are these.

- *Don't have too many targets.* 150 priorities means no priorities. Most of us can hold no more than 6 imperatives in our heads at once. Any management team charged with progressing a set of priorities will lose focus once it has more than this number. Each priority should have one or two headline targets associated with it.

- *Targets are not – they cannot be – comprehensive.* Targets cannot cover every activity. Their most important function is to ensure the organisation has a performance orientation: that *a culture of aiming high and achieving runs throughout the management process.*

- *Six targets cannot possibly express the broad range of imperatives most public sector organisations must address.* But averages should be avoided ("Our average score for these 100 targets is 8 out of 10"). They give a pseudo-scientific objectivity to a situation that inevitably includes significant under-performance. The answer is to accept that there is a hierarchy, with different management levels/teams addressing different levels of detail and different sets of targets. The more senior levels should focus on: (1) summary (not average) targets (e.g. to get the Housing function to a two star level by the end of next year); and (2) on critical issues within each of those (e.g. bring void property levels down by 50%).

- *Recognise the political reality of targets that are imposed on you.* If you do not perform against them, however good the reason, you will be seen to have failed. Work out the cheapest and quickest way to achieve the targets; and work out how, in parallel, you can invest in the longer term activities which will deliver you the substantive improvements being sought.

- *Be alert for people explaining why the measurement system is flawed* and why there is no problem with the target being missed. Look to see if, when the target was introduced, any changes were implemented in the way the organisation did business. Targets are there to address shortcomings. However flawed the targets, their arrival implies that change was needed. If no change was made, you have an issue. One definition of madness is to keep doing the same old thing in the expectation of different results.

11. The Camel House

Imagine a house where every room has been designed by a different architect. Each does their best to make their room the optimum solution for the customer; the sitting room is comfortable and warm with integrated entertainment systems; the bedrooms are shaped in line with the needs and character of family members; the kitchen is stylish, functional and easily cleaned.

But getting from room to room to door is a nightmare. Colours and styles clash between adjacent rooms. Some areas appear to be ultra modern, others cottage, others medieval. The house has to be three times as big as planned in order to accommodate the room designs, and the cost is four times budget.

The family who commissioned it hate the house the minute they step through the door. The children refuse to live there. It simply does not work and eventually has to be knocked down.

The public sector is a collection of ruggedly independent fiefdoms, barely on speaking terms, loath to cooperate; sometimes openly at war with each other. *The public, however, does not have needs which come neatly packaged*: a health need here, a social services problem there, a housing need somewhere else. *The needs of the citizen are intertwined and mutually inter-dependent.* Typically, people need solutions which are a combination of more than one service.

But the way the public sector works means that most management time is devoted to optimising the specific activities of each particular organisation or directorate. Lip service may be paid to personalised service alignment, but the reality is that performance is measured and rewarded on the basis of a fiefdom or profession.

Forward thinking Chief Executives of NHS Primary Care Trusts, when asked what single thing would most improve the health of their communities, answer, "Jobs!" Work – having a sense of purpose – is fundamental to our mental and physical well-being. So it would make sense, when investing public money in building hospitals and other health facilities, to ensure that this investment were spent in ways which delivered local jobs as well as bricks and mortar. Indeed, it would be worth paying a premium to ensure that the money did not simply bounce off the local economy into the pockets of corporations from outside the area. But our segmented approach to public service, and a fear of EU procurement legislation, prevent such joined up thinking being progressed.

I am Chair of a public-private partnership which uses the financial markets to help finance new public health buildings. You would have thought, given the fact that the public sector are key stakeholders in this partnership, that I would be coming under continual pressure to ensure that the way the money is spent, as well as what the money is used to build, is in line with local economic priorities. But no, the system seems unable to recognise and design in this connection.

You can give a camel the best knees ever designed, but if they are not compatible with the hips the camel will never run. Most of our time is spent optimising the knees rather than optimising the camel.

What point is there in jailing (at huge cost) a higher proportion of our young offenders if we are failing to invest in supporting childhoods which would reduce the rate of offending? Why, in response to various high profile child deaths, do we take a highly risk-averse approach to child abuse, removing children from their families at an early stage, when we know that the performance of Council 'looked after children' (children in care) services are so awful that we initiate generations of further abuse? Why spend so little on health promotion and so much on disease? Why regenerate the bricks and mortar of an area if the way you do it means that local people will remain disaffected (and will abuse the assets you have built)?

12. Let's Do Mission Impossible

> ### Bring the Dead Back to Life
>
> Bob was asked to undertake a strategic review of Organisation X, a failing umbrella organisation for the voluntary and community sector. He interviewed, he read, he reviewed. The core problem was clear: the organisation had been foisted upon the sector. This meant that it struggled to engage them in the issues and opportunities it was there to address. Its design was fundamentally flawed and probably unworkable. Bob also identified a range of specific operational issues. With some trepidation, he delivered his report to the board and funders. The report was well-received. So much so, in fact, that Bob was invited to work as the organisation's interim Chief Executive for 6 months to address the specific operational failings he had identified.
>
> Bob knew that he would almost certainly end up being blamed for the resultant inevitable failure. But he would be well-paid in the meantime, and be exposed to a range of senior people who could be future clients. Despite his better judgement, Bob took on the challenge. He allowed himself to think that, maybe, he could actually make this work.
>
> Six months later, exhausted, he was forced to mothball the organisation and step down. He had put his heart and soul into the task, but it had proved impossible. And he had, on the way, met many senior potential future customers. But perhaps a third of them still, to this day, see him as the man who failed.

Impossible jobs abound across the public sector. Politicians and senior civil servants usually want to make positive changes happen, but it is not always possible.

A Mission Impossible is defined in reasonable sounding terms, targets and budgets are attached, and someone takes or is given responsibility. And then, by definition, they fail. The failure may be quiet or it may be spectacular – but it is always lonely for the responsible person. All those people who offered help and support in the early stages melt away.

The blame game operates in earnest. It is in everyone's interest to allocate blame to a Mission Impossible's owner, rather than to let it fall on them. The louder you blame the other party, the less likely any of the blame is to stick to you. So the responsible person takes the hit – to reputation, earnings potential and career prospects. Where responsibility is spread across several people, either all of them become tarred by association or the underground blame allocation process is played out with energy and vigour until one version of why the failure happened emerges as received truth: one named player becomes the fall guy.

- The Child Support Agency was never going to be popular or easy. Nor was the Millennium Dome – a project with a set of objectives informed by public sector wishful thinking rather than commercial sense, and built on a site chosen for its regeneration requirement rather than its strategic location.
- The UK Borders Agency, set up to administer the ill-defined and politically fraught refugee and immigration process, will always be required to carry the can for wider failings in the system.
- The now defunct Learning & Skills Council was never likely to succeed. Given that all previous structural attempts to address the UK's skills deficit had ended in failure (so why should the LSC be any different?) it was formed by merging 80-odd robustly independent organisations. The research shows that most two-way mergers fail to deliver added value, so why would anyone think that an 80-way merger would deliver anything more than sustained in-fighting and unhappiness?

The consequence of Mission Impossible syndrome is that people with experience are reluctant to take on any risky project, organisation or task, since they know that, if it fails through no fault of their own, they will inevitably cop for the blame, with all that this implies in terms of their job. Difficult tasks end up being taken on by untried people or incompetents and, as a result, become even less likely to deliver effective results.

For the individual, there are a number of solutions to this issue. The main one is, unsurprisingly, don't take on a Mission Impossible.

How do you know if it's impossible?

First, *people will tell you*. Yet people will tell you all sorts of things are impossible simply because they know they should have done them but have not bothered and would rather you did not show up their lack of effort or insight.

So, second, *listen to your intuition*: if it tells you the task is not doable, do not allow your enthusiasm for the challenge to drown out the messages from your subconscious.

Third, *ask a range of stakeholders*, critical to the success of the assignment, whether they think it is doable. If a good number say no, or won't see you, don't do it.

And, if you *must* do it, make sure you know that the key stakeholders know that you know the game, and that in exchange for the probability you will be the fall guy, *they will guarantee to look after your long term interests*.

13. Think Like Branson!

Central government, local government, and their various agencies are called 'the public sector'. We call businesses 'the private sector'. Because these phrases look similar, we imagine that the concepts they label are themselves similar. We imagine that, like the public sector, the private sector has a degree of conformity in motivation, structure, ways of working and outlook.

In fact, the public sector itself has very little homogeneity. Though it is possible to imagine one person speaking on behalf of the sector – the Chief Cabinet Secretary, perhaps, or the leader of a civil service union – his or her ability to express a view which is consistent across the sector, except as regards the most peripheral of matters, is very limited. And the private sector is several orders of magnitude more diverse and disparate than that. On almost any given subject, therefore, there is no such thing as 'the private sector view'.

In a very real sense, the private sector is all of the people. We all trade; we all buy and sell.

For good reasons, the public sector tries to build relationships with business. The economy depends upon private enterprise; little would happen in the world of public service unless businesses were part of the mix; the roads we drive on, the food we eat, the buildings we live in happen through the activities of business people. It is right, therefore, that public sector agencies aim to take private sector views into account as they plan and implement their work. If any organisation is to work effectively it should take into account the way the world is – and our world includes businesses.

Frequently, this desire to engage with the private sector translates into the appointment of a business 'representative' to a public sector committee, advisory panel or board of directors. Their job is to speak for the private sector, to bring a business focus to the discussion. These representatives are either from a representative organisation (a trade body or the like) or a senior person from a specific business. Neither category of person is able to fulfil the desired role. The representative organisations are staffed by people whose core competence is to network and create consensus around loose imperatives. Their diverse membership does not enable them to express a focused position, even if they had the personal wherewithal. The individual business person is just that – an individual, capable of representing his or her own interests but no more able to speak on behalf of businesses as whole than any other person in the street.

The overall approach – to engage with the private sector by having a representative on a committee – is flawed. It is simply not possible to represent business as a whole this way. If business engagement is sought by a public sector agency, it must be achieved by hard graft; by detailed and ongoing dialogue between senior players from that agency and senior people from a range of relevant businesses. Engagement with representatives – at least, engagement *only* with representatives, rather than through them – is lazy and ineffective.

There is often a second objective for bringing business people into the public sector fold. Politicians and many senior public sector figures, who often have little private sector experience, are seduced by the idea that private sector ways of working have much to teach the public sector. "The private sector would never put up with all this inefficiency", they say, or "Who is our customer?" Business representatives are brought in to contribute their management expertise to the task at hand.

It is true to say that many such business people will have much to contribute. But the public sector is a different world, without the simplicity at the heart of private sector transactions. All business decisions boil down to the attempt to maximise a return on investment, enabled by the common currency which is finance. This philosophy underlies and informs all business transactions; this is the job of business. But the public sector rarely has that degree of simplicity: there are no definitive models available to identify if the greater social/economic/political return will be achieved by investing in more heart transplants or in more special schools. In the public sector, *decisions will always be based on faith, hope and politics* as well as calculation. The core skills of a business person – to be able to focus on the areas where the return is greatest – are not the whole story in the public sector.

Government agencies can go badly wrong if they are seduced by the interventions of a powerful business person. And business people can be badly distracted and corrupted through involvement in public sector work – to the detriment of their business and the economy as a whole.

14. Distraction Therapy

Instead of solving the problem, senior public sector players will often do something else which looks as if it is helpful but actually is a distraction. Since this is a book about problem solving, rather than how to avoid problem solving, I don't intend to dwell on these (admittedly, often effective) techniques. But you might find it helpful to add them to your theoretical armoury, if only to spot when someone else is employing them.

Restructure

When there are problems, the problems are not usually a result of organisation structures. Organisation structures look like systems maps, architectural drawings or machine layouts. As a result, there is an easy assumption that, if the design is changed, the functionality will improve.

The truth is that organisation structure diagrams give as good an impression of the functioning of an organisation as family trees give you insight into the inner life of a family. There is a connection between the two, but it is not a close connection. Reorganisations typically do not make wholesale changes to: (1) the people doing the job in the front line; (2) the basic approaches (processes) taken to the core tasks; or (3) the *raison d'être* of the organisation. They do look as if the leaders/board/members/Ministers are taking tough decisions and showing decisive leadership, but really they are doing nothing of the sort.

This is not to say that reorganisations are not occasionally necessary. The point is that organisations are complex organic networks of living people. Typically, the work is done because of the organic nature of the links between people, rather than because of formal reporting lines. Any disruption to those organic links caused by ill-thought through restructuring, can (and often does) have detrimental effects on the real ways of working.

The Learning and Skills Council was invented to replace the Further

Education Funding Council and the Training and Enterprise Councils, whose employees had spent a decade learning how to work with an imperfect system to get things done (some well, some not so well). The change was like uprooting and replanting a tree – it may look the same but its roots are damaged and it may struggle to survive. Now, a decade later, the LSC is itself being restructured and replaced. Will the successor arrangements be any more effective?

The right approach is to spend good, inclusive time (with employees, customers, partners) working out the realities of why the organisation's performance is deficient; to build, again through an inclusive dialogue, organic answers to the problems which are highlighted; then, and only then, to reshape reporting lines (and replace staff), if necessary, to allow those solutions to blossom.

Mapping and Gapping

The issues which the public sector is there to solve (disadvantage, illness, discrimination, housing etc) are complex and often inter-dependent. In most cases, leaders and managers will never have perfect information on which they can act. Decisions must be made, of course, on the basis of the best information available – but the point is that decisions must, at some point, be made. It is too easy for risk-averse public servants to make no decision at all: to call for 'mapping and gapping' (ie better research into the issues) in order to inform a better decision later. In the meantime, while a decision has not been made, people suffer.

This is not a call for irresponsibility. The public sector should be considered and careful in its decision making. But leaders and managers should also be aware of the consequences of *not* making a decision, and weigh those factors in the balance before calling for further data. If a meteorite is due to hit the earth in a month's time, and the only solution is to fire a rocket at it now, we had best fire the rocket now rather than wait for an improved analysis of its weight and composition. In the end, we are in danger of forgetting that a core management responsibility is to exercise judgement.

Build the Manual
Too much public sector time is spent trying to build the machinery of public services, rather than letting the front line people get on with the service activity. Committees spend hours defining and refining their terms of reference and governance arrangements, rather than governing. Managers spend time and consultant days defining processes rather than overseeing the quality of the services provided. Contract managers spend their time drafting, amending and reviewing contracts rather than engaging with the resultant delivery.

There is no point in having an operating manual and no machine. And, as we have explored earlier, it is questionable whether any kind of machine analogy is appropriate anyway. If running a public service is more like tending a garden than operating a machine, the management challenge is more akin to tending, nurturing and pruning than it is to engineering.

Documents Not Relationships
When public sector managers and leaders don't know what to do, they require a document to be produced. Most often their time would be better spent going out and listening to those directly affected.

Organisations As Solutions
If public sector managers and leaders don't know what to do about a really significant problem they will create an organisation (or a department) to own it. This often has the effect of allowing the mainstream services, which should have flexed to address the problem, to continue to ignore it on the basis that it is not theirs to worry about.

Organisations are never solutions. *Solutions are based on a different way of doing things*. If the new way of doing things requires the invention of a new organisation, so be it: but it is not the newness of the organisation which is the determinant of success. New organisations, with new chiefs wanting to display how they are different from what came before, can actually exacerbate the problem by alienating the people who know the issues and customers well and who have invested much of themselves, under successive regimes, in trying to make a difference.

Customer Relationship Management

Most public sector organisations work with clients or customers: the public. And there is a general sense that, if only we could have better information about our individuals customers, just like the supermarkets do, we could provide them with a better, more joined up service. To get that better information, the argument goes, we must invest in a Customer Relationship Management (CRM) system: a computerised means of capturing information from each customer transaction, so enabling us to make more informed management decisions across organisations.

The logic of this thinking is sound and the approach can work. More often, though, large sums of money are spent on CRM-based IT, with project plans that slip and slip, and which are in danger of obstructing the customer-based work in the meantime.

The problem is that relationships are at the heart of what good public sector services are about (hospital visits, job seekers, training) and relationships cannot be captured in an IT system. *Front line public servants with a good relationship building outlook are typically those who are least likely to engage with, or to want to engage with, a CRM system.* And out-of-date data quickly becomes worthless data. Managers essentially have a choice: between a powerful CRM system operated by staff who do not care, and a caring, engaging team whose knowledge of the customer can only be understood through on-going, supportive management relationships.

The long running and over-budget NHS patient records management system is just the most well-known of this numerous family of obstructive solutions.

PART FOUR

TRANSACTIONS NOT RELATIONSHIPS

Public sector problems and solutions all concern people and the relationships between them. Yet we have come to behave as if what matters is the action, the transaction, the particular exchange. And in some cases – for instance, an appendix operation – it is undoubtedly the case that the transaction between surgeon and patient is more important than the relationship.

But the relationship between the patient and the GP potentially stretches over a lifetime and will be more effective (in terms of both long term patient health and other social positives) the better it is. The relationship of trust that builds up between a social worker and a service user is more important – and more powerful – than any one visit. *But the emphasis on visit reports, checklists and process conformance places the value of the session above the value of the relationship*, and results in frequent changes of personnel – which can result, in turn, in the further alienation of the service user.

We must recognise that *transactions and relationships are of **equal** significance* to public service: that neither can take place without the other; that neither can be fully effective if the other is poor.

15. I am the Spanner, You are the Nut

> The nut holds the wheel on the car. It sees itself as important to the wheel, the car, the driver and their journey. It has a complex and varied life.
>
> The spanner sits in the toolbox. It thinks it is the most important thing in the life of the nut.

Some public servants have the unpleasant habit of seeing the world from the point of view of the spanner. Consultants, social workers, teachers, regeneration practitioners, managers, politicians – a good proportion of people in public service – see their work as fundamental to the survival and well-being of their clients/voters/service users/patients/students. They see those customers principally as the recipients of the support they provide, in much the same way that a spanner must see itself as important to a nut.

In reality, most people's happiness and success results from their wider lives; their relationships with the people around them; their family, neighbours, workmates, and friends. They think about the public sector rarely, even if they work in it. They are complex and muddled, as we all are. If they are public sector service customers they are complex, muddled service users of multiple services. So when they meet with a public servant, there is often a mismatch of perspectives. *The service customer sees the meeting as peripheral to his or her life, troubling, and strangely narrow in scope. The public servant sees the meeting as defining the service user; as central to that person's existence.*

The parent of a deaf child will quickly tire, for instance, of being required to tell the story of their child and its deafness dozens and dozens of times per year – to every new GP, consultant, social worker, teacher, teacher of the deaf, audiometrist, speech therapist, cochlea implant specialist, and nurse the condition causes them to meet. The professional, on the other hand, will feel quite reasonable in opening by asking for this information since it will help them provide an effective episode of care. The parent sees this pattern as an irritating feature of the family's relationship with the service they receive; the individual professional sees it as a necessary part of the support encounter they deliver. The truth lies in a balance between the two. The family should learn, and be helped to learn, how best to work with the professionals. Each professional should recognise the family's perspective, and find ways to demonstrate their attempts to connect. And the system should be designed to allow and encourage continuity of contact; to place emphasis on the development of the clinician's interpersonal as well as technical skills.

The problems addressed by the public sector are, necessarily, hugely important; including health, well-being, and survival in all its forms. But most of the public sector's interventions are of limited impact.

- A heart operation may extend a life but will not address the forty year old social habits that caused the disease.
- A college may offer an NVQ course but will not provide the motivation which the student needs to complete it.
- The transport system may support a thriving economy, but does not create it.
- The local authority's community strategy is a document, not a community. Public services need to be humble, if they are to make a real contribution.

I have three over-arching rules for public services. These are:

1. Don't make the problem worse
2. Don't do something irrelevant
3. Don't ignore your heart.

A significant proportion of what is done in the public sector has the effect, either in the short or long term, of *worsening the situation* it attempts to solve – yet we keep doing it. When we have tried a solution and it has not worked, our standard response is *to try harder rather than to try something else.*

- We build social housing in ways that lock in disadvantage, extending the need for social housing.
- We develop qualifications based on outdated competences and hold back innovation.
- We imprison young offenders and they learn how to offend better.
- We impose targets on hospitals and get higher infection rates.
- We deliver education as if the world of knowledge were effectively finite and static, rather than infinite, complex and rapidly developing.

The third rule, *Don't ignore your heart*, means two things. It asks that each of us, as individuals, watch our own health and well being (literally, the condition of our own heart muscle) while we work in public service. The task is bigger than any one of us, it will take every ounce of effort you have, and will rarely say thank you. Most people who work in or around the public sector are highly committed to what they do. Those who are committed, and who are (or are capable of being) competent, must watch that they do not burn themselves out and become either dead or cynical. (Those who are not committed and competent should go work somewhere else).

The rule also points at the fact that we should be prepared to be emotional as well as logical; that *we should listen to our own intuition* concerning what is right. Often we take action on the basis of a seemingly logical argument which flies in the face of what we feel is the right option. But the logic turns out to have been inadequate: we would have done better listening to our own inclinations. This is not always the case, of course: but this is the way it works more often than we allow ourselves to recognise. How many lives would be saved, how many families would be happier, if social workers were encouraged and supported to pay attention to their intuition, rather than to targets, checklists and risk-averse systems?

In short, *judgement* is key to the effective delivery of public service. In the wake of the Baby P case, Children's Services across the country tightened up on their procedures, requiring that children were removed from their families at the smallest indication of risk, overruling the judgement of front line professionals. The consequence? – more children in care. And 'looked after children' (ie those who are looked after by the state) are many times more likely to experience educational underperformance and general dysfunction in later life, including problems in parenting their own children.

So the potential consequence of overruling front line intuition in this case is that we initiate a significantly greater risk of abuse for the next generation of children.

15. The High Rise People

By the 1950s, poor people have been living in urban slums for generations. Overcrowded and with inadequate sanitation, the slum areas spawned disease and under-achievement.

The planners and architects determined to clear the slums; to replace them with bright new housing, functional, efficient: high rise flats, "villages in the sky". They shipped people out of the slums into the new flats, knocked down the slums, and gave each other awards for their cleverness. And went back to their detached homes in the suburbs.

The high rise flats proved to be unpleasant and unnatural places to live. People felt isolated and detached. Dysfunctional families no longer were kept under social control; their impact on their neighbours became extreme. The health challenges of the slums were replaced by mental health problems and by crime. The physical environment rapidly decayed.

What do people feel makes an attractive village? Typically, they will be drawn to a place that has an organic feel: the houses come in different shapes and sizes, the roads follow the natural curves of a river, there is tumble of plants, trees and hedgerows. Yet housing developments in the latter part of the twentieth century were characterised by straight lines, by intentionality, by utility. The worst examples were the high rise blocks of flats, lacking the fundamentally organic features of a real village – and failing, as a result.

We do the equivalent of building high rise across the public sector; in health, social services, skills – across the board. It is what happens when we see people as units, as commercial entities with finite sets of needs with whom we can develop and sign contracts to ensure those needs are fulfilled.

If a person is no more than a bundle of essentially definable needs, the challenge is straightforward: to list those needs then meet them within economically viable parameters. To do so, we need expertise; expertise in identifying needs and expertise in designing solutions. In such a world, the expert has primacy.

This is the logic that leads to building High Rise. It is the logic that leads to women being told to give birth lying flat on their back with their legs in callipers; that leads to industrial skills delivery machines (our poorer quality colleges and universities) churning out people with qualifications but no understanding; that leads to the welfare dependency trap. It is why we have a health service which cannot possibly meet demand, social services and welfare expenditure bigger than the economy of Belgium, and a whole class of people feeling subject to, rather than the shapers of, their lives.

Why do we continue to build High Rise? It's partly due to our obsession with sequential-analytical thinking. The view is that, if people have needs, we must be able to list those needs, cluster them together, and act on them – it's compelling logic. But the problem is that not all of a person's needs can be listed like this. People are not like washing machines, with distinct and measurable characteristics, categorisable according to size or price or prestige. People do not start by knowing what they need. They find out their preferences – they *form* their preferences – by experiment, by trial and error, by conversation. They can be enthused by something they never would have known they needed; that no one could have predicted they wanted.

And the most fundamental need which underpins all this is *the need for involvement, for ownership*. However right a solution might seem to a person, if they have not been involved in identifying it as their solution, they are not likely to be happy with it.

How about getting disaffected young men to build their own homes, rather than provide them with social housing that they will abuse? In fact, why is the social housing system not set up so that affordable houses can only be built by those who need a job, skills and a house?

This is not the same as offering people choice, though choice is one way of spreading ownership. Having choice over which hospital will conduct your vasectomy is of little use if you have no information to enable you to select, and no expertise to enable you to form a judgement. Choice in this setting can look like a facsimile of involvement, drawing attention to your real lack of involvement, and therefore becoming counter-productive.

The fundamental solution is not choice, but involvement. The more that people are part of the process of creating solutions to their needs, the more the solution is likely to work, even if it is not the best on-paper solution. The problem with involvement is that it is expensive: it requires person by person attention to detail; it requires listening and time; it requires humility from the experts (medical consultants, architects, health planners, college principals) who are used to being remote and respected. It requires significant up-front investment from budgets that are too small to allow for it. And yet the price of a lack of involvement is much bigger, though paid later and, typically, by different budget holders. If we do not involve young children more in the content and style of their education we condemn a significant proportion of them to under-achievement, and a hard core minority to a dysfunctional life of crime, violence and dysfunction – all very expensive for society as a whole.

Building high rise is what we do when we forget *the importance of emotions, belonging and respect* in the human psyche. We all know that these things are important to ourselves, as individuals, but we often struggle to accept the significance of anything other than functional needs to other people. Research consistently shows that this is particularly true for young people who place considerable emphasis on the "respect" (or lack of it) that they are shown by the system; caring more about this than about the content of the service itself.

17. We Are All In It Together!

One of the reasons why our public sector is so full of problems is that it is staffed by many Problem Breeders. These are people who have become expert at turning two problems into fifteen; at nurturing rather than removing problems; at maintaining high levels of public expenditure on flawed programmes that do little more – and sometimes much less – than address the symptoms of the problem rather than the cause.

Few Problem Breeders are malicious or deliberately obstructive. Most are intelligent, well-meaning and thorough. Many believe they are working about as hard as it is possible to work, and have vaguely egalitarian tendencies. It is probably a good thing that public money is spent on keeping them off the street – though many might be a good deal happier, wealthier and more fulfilled if they were part of the enterprise economy. The country certainly would be.

Problem Breeder tendencies are exacerbated by the system. The UK's public sector can be seen as a mechanism – a wide variety of mechanisms – established over time to address specific issues. The snag is that, once organisational-type mechanisms have been set up, they can be replaced but it is very hard to get rid of them. The people who operate them have a vested interest in their continued existence. Politicians are afraid to close something down which, even if it is ineffective, at least looks as if it is doing something to address a known issue.

The most that happens is that the organisation is restructured or replaced. This looks politically decisive and positive, and is usually accompanied by an attempt to refocus and improve. Yet the same Problem Breeders end up running it, *because they created the vocabulary by which the problem is described*.

The people who appear best equipped to deal with the country's skills deficit, for instance, are those who have for years been trading in the language of skills, running training providers or the funding systems associated with them. The fundamental assumption underpinning this sector is that an investment in skills will pay significant returns to the economy. This assumption then leads to a qualifications industry, with significant effort and money expended on raising the numbers of NVQs, GCSEs and degrees out in the world.

Though some of this spending will help in the quest for greater competitiveness, its effect is much diminished by the flawed thinking which characterises the approach. Economic effectiveness (personal, corporate or national) does not result from skills, it results from *skilled people.*

Here's an analogy. It may be the case that your house will sell for a higher price if all the cars in your street are well-polished. If you went out and bought car wax for all your neighbours, one or two might use it, and there might be a slight and occasional effect on the smartness of the street. But the impact on house prices would be negligible. To achieve significant impact, you would need to change the outlook, the culture, of the neighbourhood, so that people would feel a collective need to keep things tidy, so that neighbours would help each other do so, so that peer pressure and social control would be exerted on those who did not polish, tidy and trim. People have to want to use the polish. And if you simply decided to polish their cars for them? Well you could, but it would take a good chunk of time every week; and the money you could make by using that time in another way would far exceed the impact on your house price.

Skills are not entities in their own right, separate from the people who have them – any more than the shine of a well-polished car can exist without the car. Investing in skills is like investing in polish. Skills don't change much on their own. They are only part of the economic development story, and probably not the place to start. But if you see life through a skills prism, every problem looks like a skills problem.

The real fault lies with us, the voters. In the same way that no government finds it easy to remove red tape – health and safety legislation, for instance – because the media would get us all up in arms about the inevitable new risks we would be exposed to, so politicians are pilloried for a lack of care when they close down a particular government programme or function. You get the government you deserve.

There are no **easy** solutions. Here are some thoughts.

- We need those talented people who are stifled and suppressed by their jobs in the public sector to work as innovators in the private sector (since, without a private sector, you have no economy, no tax revenue and no welfare state). So we need a more efficient and focused public sector that sucks fewer of them in.
- We need to reward public sector people who solve problems, rather than nurture them, so that they are motivated to *bring their support activity to an end*, rather than grow it.
- We need to get into the habit of closing two initiatives down every time we launch a new one.
- We need to check, at all times, that we are 'thinking beyond the problem'; that we are checking that we are not seeing both challenge and solution through too narrow a prism.
- We need to watch out for, and get rid of, the Problem Breeders.

18. Make Artificial Friends

<table>
<tr><td>

What is Friendship?

Do you remember, as a child, an adult saying to you something like, "Why don't you make friends with Johnny? He's a nice boy, and we know his Mum and Dad." And the sinking feeling of dread that this engendered? How could you tell your parents that Johnny was the weirdest boy in the playground?

You know, as a child, that friendships don't work that way. Friendship does not happen because it is logical that it should; it cannot be imposed, according to a set of rules, from the outside. Though people generally feel happier in their lives if they have strong friendship groups, good friends cannot be procured in a shop, or arranged by lawyers.

</td></tr>
</table>

Partnerships in the public sector are reckoned a Good Thing. Sometimes it seems that everything is supposed to be done through partnership. But organisational partnerships are like friendships. Friendship is at the heart of what it is to be human; it is the foundation of a strong society. We see friendship as an undiluted positive.

But what of *artificial friendships*? Most of us would find the concept worrying, even abhorrent.

Artificial friendships can work: some charitable organisations bring together willing volunteers with, for instance, young mothers who are struggling to cope; some may evolve into real friendship. The priest or doctor may be a friend-substitute in times of need. But artificial friendships entered into for self-interested reasons or commercial gain can be corrosive and damaging. So partnership, when it is encouraged (or required) from the outside is like artificial friendship. It *can* work. It can become *true* partnership. But the participants will have to work to make it real.

Every area of the UK is now required to have a Local Strategic Partnership (LSP); a coming together of the council with the police, fire, local health, skills and other services. Some of these undoubtedly add value and get things done. The vast majority decline into no more than a series of stale meetings in which the participants focus on providing performance numbers to central government and finding ways to ensure they don't have to give up any budget to the collective. The LSP Director becomes a disillusioned whipping boy or an administrator; the citizen sees evidence of nothing other than more obscure meetings.

Why is partnership so emphasised? It comes down to the problems we are trying to solve. Customers' problems are not neatly packaged. They rarely relate to, or are solved by, one service – or even one public sector organisation. A child suffering from abuse has an above average chance of suffering from a host of other problems – poverty, poor educational achievement, wider health issues.

So the good solutions tend to be where multiple services and multiple agencies work together to provide joined up solutions, specific to the issue and people involved. This joined up working has come to be known as Partnership. And Partnership, as we all know, is a good thing.

But there is a logical fallacy here. Here's the logic: good things happen when there are partnerships, therefore everyone should be required to have a partnership. This is akin to saying, all footballers have nice legs, therefore if I have nice legs I will be good at football.

The point is that partnerships may be necessary for good solutions, but they are not sufficient. Other factors also need to be present. And, anyway, you can have a partnership that is a bad partnership. Bad partnerships can actually make things worse, by draining resources away from the task of basic delivery, service by service, organisation by organisation. People who are forced into partnership will not often make good partners.

Ah yes, say the policy makers, but what we want is a Good Partnership. Good Partnerships always deliver solutions.

So how do they suggest we recognise Good Partnerships? Answers usually come in two forms. The first is circular and unhelpful. It basically says that Good Partnerships are those that produce results. This statement does not add much value if what you are looking for is guidance on how to get one off the ground. The second type of answer proffered takes the form of that favourite policy maker construct: a checklist or framework. These will list a range of good practice points concerning process (e.g. clarity concerning terms of reference, clear governance, the management of action points, shared vision and objectives, etc), and supplement this with homilies concerning participant satisfaction and honesty. Neither type of answer gets to the heart of the issue. They do no more than define nice-leggedness in more detail.

The problem in all this is the frame of reference. The public sector discusses partnership as if it were a machine or a building. People perhaps think that building a partnership is a bit like putting up a tent when we have lost the instructions, but the approach to getting it up will basically be the same as that of the family next door, if we could but copy them.

Partnerships are not like tents. They are more like families. And families, unlike tents, do not exist for a particular purpose. They exist for many purposes – and for no purpose at all, other than that is the way we are. And families do not perform well or badly. They may be strong or not so strong. They may even be dysfunctional. But families can never be perfect, will always have internal tensions, and must always work at it. Family members are all responsible for keeping the family on the track, for flexing to each other's needs, characteristics and hang ups; for standing up for other family members.

The processes of partnerships, like their published terms of reference, or their governance arrangements, are just the externally observable features. Judging the strength of a partnership on the basis of these characteristics would be like judging a family on the cleanliness of its carpets or the weed free nature of its garden. There may be a link – but there may not. Many strong, loving, 'successful' families are chaotic.

So, if we accept the analogy, what *does* make for a strong partnership?

Genuine partnerships between public sector organisations work because people on the front line have *the space and support to work together*. Such partnerships do not result from top level meetings and strategic plans, but from a recognition, by middle managers and the people at the coal face that they can do a better job working alongside others.

- Containing crime is easier for the police if they work with schools and social services.
- Reducing obesity is easier for a Primary Care Trust if it works with the Council's Leisure Services function.
- Job Centres find it easier to connect with the workless if they build links with housing associations.

This all requires managers and professionals within those organisations to practice the softer skills of partnership, and be given the space and support by senior management to do so.

Listening. Understanding. Realising that my needs are not your needs. Working out how best to give you what you want in a way that gives me what I want. Compromising when this is not possible. Knowing that, whatever else happens, we are better together than apart. Believing this as hard as we can. Above all else, working to understand the personalities of the people in the room; their enthusiasms, the basis on which they will be judged back in their own organisation. Finding ways to love them. Yes, to love them. Not romantically, but as fellow humans: finding it in our hearts to honour the person that they are.

Of course, this is not always possible. Sometimes partnerships cannot work, just as, sometimes, families can not work. But, most of the time, we can try a good deal harder than most of us do.

Having said that checklists are not the answer to good partnership working, I set out some basic good practice prompts in Part Five: evidence, perhaps, of my own ability to live with ambiguity (or inconsistency!)

19. The Non-Exec is Always Right

Many public sector organisations have boards of directors, comparable to larger businesses, with non-executive members sitting alongside the top team. They may be there to improve governance; to bring a dispassionate, or private sector, perspective; to connect with complementary organisations; or to bring a local view. But non-executives can be a headache. Either they do nothing, and add no value, or they do something, and get in the way.

What needs to be understood by all players, not least the non-executive himself or herself, is this: the non-executive is just that – *not* **executive** – a person who is not there to *do* things. Their role is primarily to hold others to account. More specifically, the non-executive responsibilities are to ensure that:

- The organisation has a compelling and proper approach to undertaking its responsibilities;
- The Chief Executive is making good progress in pursuing that approach.

Everything else either contributes to these two or is irrelevant to the role.

In ensuring that the organisation has an effective strategy, non-executives may find themselves involved in the design and implementation of processes and procedures, in the development of business plans, in dialogues with government or other organisations. But it is important to understand that this involvement is always non-executive: it is there to choose between options presented, to reject bad thinking, to ensure connections between people are made that otherwise might not be made.

*It is not to **create** the strategy; it is not to tell the Chief Executive what to* *do or how to do it. It is not to run the show.*

In ensuring the Chief Executive is making progress, the non-executive role is not to provide him or her with detailed instructions; it is not to do the job for the Chief Executive; it is not to select the team to work with the Chief Executive. Too often do we see boards of organisations telling the Chief Executive what to do based on their experience elsewhere. This always leads to problems. The Chief Executive must be accountable for the overall performance and staff of the organisation. If there is a failure (of performance, probity or conformance), the Chief Executive must take responsibility for resolving it. But if the decision which led to that failure was made, not by the Chief Executive, but by the non-executives, the Chief Executive can rightly disown responsibility. The board immediately loses its leverage over the business. Who does it now hold to account? And if it dismisses the Chief Executive for under-performance it will rightly lose an unfair dismissal claim. The non-executives are there to determine **what** is done: it is for the executive to determine **how**.

Non-executives can help the Chief Executive make decisions, recruit staff, build the strategy. But the business must at all times be led and managed by the Chief Executive: he or she must at all times feel responsible for what is going on.

And the non-executives must be ready to sack the Chief Executive when he or she is found wanting. It is not unusual for Chief Executives to want non-executives to be closely involved in operational decisions. This can be quite a seductive move for the non-exec: they are usually effective people, which is why they have been asked to help, used to making things happen and to getting involved in detail. But such involvement must be resisted, other than at times of crisis (for instance, in replacing the Chief Executive). It **always** results in muddled thinking and an undermining of the essential accountability of the executive team.

20. Voters Made Me Wise

Members of government, local authority councillors and elected officials in general are really *a special type of non-executive*. They differ from the standard non-executive in two important respects. Firstly, they are more visibly to blame when things go wrong. Secondly, and this is linked to the previous point, they find it even more tempting to interfere in how things are done. The role of a politician in power is, therefore, always fraught. They are required by their role to make decisions and to be held to account for so doing by the electorate. Yet operational decisions really ought to be taken by the employed experts through an accountable executive management structure.

Here are some rules of conduct for elected members. If they are followed, there will still be trouble – but it will be significantly less than if they are not.

- Be clear **what** you want doing. Let the paid employees work out options for **how** it might be done.
- Express your views on how it should be done, if you must. But do not prevent the executive from developing the options, making recommendations and – here is the important bit – taking responsibility for progressing what is decided.
- Do not let the executive seduce you into making their detailed 'how to' decisions for them. They are paid to take responsibility for these. Ensure they do so.
- If the executive makes bad decisions consistently, or will not produce a sensible set of options, replace them.
- Work with and through the management hierarchy. It will be tempting to cut through the red tape and give direct instructions to lower levels of staff. Doing so will quickly result in poor delivery performance as accountability becomes blurred and priorities are undermined.

- If the only way to get things done is to give direct instructions to lower level staff, get rid of the higher level staff.
- Remember that you know less about how to do things than the executive. They are the professionals. Just because they work for you does not mean they know less than you. They are not there to make you feel superior. If they do know less than you, replace them.
- Be humble when you take the credit, be generous when you take the blame. The electorate will respect you. Your executive will love you and give you higher levels of protection than you deserve.

21. Failure Intolerance

People with a private sector background will tend to berate the public sector for being risk-averse: they will draw attention to the fact that risk is the way that progress is made. They are right. *Risk is necessary to progress.* This is especially true in the public sector, where the tough problems are resistant to standard solutions. *We must take risk if we are to find new answers.*

But the private sector is not particularly good at risk taking. Most people in the private sector work for someone else; they are trained to do a job rather than to take risk. People who berate the public sector are rarely entrepreneurs themselves; typically they operate in highly structured environments where 'risk' is actually about following well established investment frameworks.

Most commercial entrepreneurs are good, not at incurring personal risk, but at finding ways of risking other people's money and minimising the risks to themselves. There is no inherent virtue in taking risks: the virtue comes from understanding risk; from containing it as much as possible; from assessing scale of risk against potential reward; and from taking a risk when the returns look good. Good entrepreneurs are not addicted and undisciplined gamblers. And neither should public sector managers be. What is needed is risk management, not risk-orientation or risk avoidance.

The problem is that it is this last characteristic, risk-avoidance, which can dominate the public sector working environment. This is unsurprising given the public attitude to failure and to mishap: that both can and should be avoided by good management; when anything goes wrong, someone somewhere should have been in a position to anticipate and prevent it.

This is, of course, infantile nonsense. We all know, in our daily lives, that few things ever go as we hope. But there is an overpowering sense, perhaps resulting from our long exposure to the (generally positive) welfare state, that somehow 'they' should make sure that nothing can ever go wrong. A child dies and it is the Council's fault. A town floods and it the Environment Agency's fault. A train de-rails and it is the fault of the government's approach to rail privatisation. An epidemic kicks off and the NHS is to blame. A person contracts incurable cancer and NICE is pilloried for blocking the NHS from purchasing a hugely expensive wonder drug.

Ideally, the public sector as a whole should take a more mature approach to risk: recognising that risk is a fact of life; that for progress to be made risks have to be taken; and that people who try and fail are to be valued since (1) they do at least try, unlike many people; and (2) they are less likely to fail next time, since they will almost certainly have learnt some valuable lessons. But for the public sector to adopt this realistic risk attitude, society at large would have to do so: and what hope is there of that?

If society cannot be changed, public sector risk systems can be made smarter. We can all adopt a more risk-managed approach in practice rather than just paying lip service to the concept, whilst avoiding risk like the plague. This means learning from the real private sector, not from the cartoon version of the private sector entrepreneur we are given by the private sector manager. It means creating frameworks within which quantified risks can be taken.

It means *becoming used to a prototyping approach*, trying a number of different approaches to the same problem in parallel, rigorously assessing which ones work; stopping the ones that fail and doing more of the ones that succeed. And then doing the same with the next problem, or the next time the same problem manifests itself, since *public sector problems shift and evolve according to the virtues and vices of the people involved with them.*

22. Sack the Troublemaker

Such is the risk-averse orientation that has developed in contemporary life that much of what we do in the public sector is trammelled by guidelines, processes and constraints. Activities which any sensible person would join up are undertaken separately, according to the rules and regulatory regimes to which they 'belong'. Every once in a while we notice the absurdity of the arrangement and try to do something about it. It was recognised that the death of little Victoria Climbié at the hands of her aunt, for instance, could probably have been prevented had the various professionals who came into contact with her spoken with each other.

Often we set out to encourage a more joined up system – but end up with an approach that simply establishes new divisions between new bundles of activity.

A small number of individuals in the public sector refuse to play by the rules. Some of these are simply destructive and must be shown the exit. The others are desirable mavericks, able to follow common sense, build alliances across functions and take risks to produce results. The trouble is that the two types can be difficult to distinguish. Risks, by their nature, don't always come off.

Mavericks – good or bad – can have a destabilising effect on the rest of an organisation: people ask why they should continue to follow the rules when the maverick is so able to break them with apparent impunity. And no organisation can consist entirely of mavericks. But mavericks are necessary if the organisation is to rise above the procedural and mundane. They can't be developed, they can only be identified, cosseted and motivated. But it's a risky game.

This is what works, when working with mavericks.

- Kick out bad ones the minute you start thinking they might be bad and have just cause to do so.
- Keep the good ones very close to you. Put time and effort into building their personal loyalty to you. If they don't care about you, get rid of them.
- Steal other people's mavericks if you don't have any of your own.
- Expect their utility to last no more than four years. Be loyal to them and help them find their next role. They will prove useful to you later.
- Drop them like a stone, however effective they are, if they break the rules. Remember, their job is to sail close to the wind, to stick to the letter not spirit of the law. They will always be tempted to inch just that little bit too far towards the devil. If they do, they must go. Or you will have to.

So how do you recognise an effective maverick? Well, for that I am afraid there are few rules. In my experience, they will be brilliant networkers, with a strong ideological commitment to public service, combining huge arrogance and humility in equal measure, with a good gut feel for numbers but little interest in detail. If you think you might be one yourself, you are probably not. You would anyway probably be at the local, drinking beer with the committee chair, rather than reading this.

23. I Have the Gift of Leadership

In the end, many of the nastiest, most intractable organisational or partnership problems in public service are the result of ego or personality clashes. And when these are unaddressed for a period, when the systems around them adapt and institutionalise the scar tissue, the problems can drag on for years at great expense to the public purse and the intended beneficiaries of the service in question. I know a large council in which two directors of major directorates, with functions that closely impact on each other, dislike each other intensely. Their antipathy means that the major initiatives of one will almost certainly be obstructed by the other. Their inability to be in the same room as each other means that it is difficult to progress even the smallest administrative issue. A major priority for the council as a whole continues to be held up by nothing more than a personality clash.

These clashes are the stuff of history books, art, culture and the whole of human history. I am not about to claim that the solution lies in a few bullet points and wise words. But there are some basic principles which should inform any response.

- **Strip your ego out of the equation**
  Whatever else you do, you must remember that you are not paid to have your ego stroked: you are here to deliver real improvements for those who need it most. Taking a situation personally and reacting as if your organisation were your fiefdom are absolutely no-go areas. When tempted to take a situation personally, the effective public sector manager looks, with interest, to see what it is about the situation (and, perhaps, the issues in the other party) which have elicited that response; what that illustrates about the underlying issues; how the emotions of the situation can be exploited to help move it forward progressively and in ways which don't damage the fragile egos of others.

- **Win the war, not the battle**

  Conceding defeat quickly on one issue can allow significant progress to be made on a range of others. Public service, and public service career building, is a long game. So play it long.

- **It's about people, stupid**

  It is people who cause the problems and it is people who will solve them. Getting key players together in a room, hiring a good facilitator who can make progress whilst keeping the tone light – this works. Sounds obvious? Yes. But how often is it done? Call it a Long Range Strategy Workshop and no one need ever know.

PART FIVE

SOLVING THE PROBLEMS

The public servant's task, whatever the challenge, is to *contain the problem in the short term while working to solve it in the long term*; to work on it as if he were a scientist watching a Petri dish while also engaging with it as if she were a participant; to do what looks good while doing what works. The answers, therefore, are rarely simple.

In general terms, the solution to having a more effective public sector lies in the development of a greater get-things-done orientation. This is, in other words, *enterprise*. Not risk-taking, profit-oriented, self-serving behaviour, but an individual and organisational willingness to understand, think, and act in ways that respond to the particulars of the issue.

24. Simple Problems Analysis

Most public sector problems are not, of course, self-generated. But many of them have distinctive public sector characteristics, which give them a particular flavour or character, and which mean that the solutions themselves – if they are to work – must respond appropriately.

The vast majority of public sector problems are small in scale and amenable to treatment by sensible, sensitive people as part of their regular role. The fact that many are not resolved, that they fester and turn into complex issues, results from the fact that simple problem analysis is not expected from – sometimes not allowed from – many of our public servants; the same individuals who would naturally adopt such approaches in their private lives. Simple problems should be assessed through a standard logical process which scopes and clarifies the nature of the problem and the best possible approach to solving it.

These simple public sector problems differ in no important respects from any other problems. There is plenty of standard problem solving literature for those who need to improve this fundamentally important human skill. But here is a summary checklist which should act as a basic framework.

1. Define the problem
Start by asking and answering the following questions:

- What does the problem look like?
- Who suffers? Who benefits?
- What is the scale?
- What are the causes?
- What are the consequences if it is not resolved?
- What is the timescale?

2. Define the solution or success criteria

On the basis of the answers to the preceding questions, the problem solver should be able to answer, or to find a way of answering, the following:

- How will we know what is a good solution? What are the criteria by which a good solution will be judged?
- What should be the process of approval for a possible solution?
- Does everyone who should be worried about the problem know that there is a problem?
- What should we do to ensure they know?

3. Generate options

Having clarified and scoped the issue, and generated a clearer understanding of the issue we face, the problem solver should now be in a position to think about the range of possible responses. This requires the following actions.

- List possible solutions.
- Get other interested parties to help list solutions.
- Cluster possible solutions.
- Flesh possible solutions out, particularly with reference to scale and investment.

4. Judge the options

Having dispassionately gone through the preceding steps, which have therefore resulted in a thorough and objective assessment of the issue and solutions from all angles, now it is time to form a view on the relative merits of each possible approach. This requires the following actions.

- Apply the judgement criteria to each option.
- Rank the options.
- Review the ranking.
- Rework the judgement.

- Enlist the help of interested parties in judging and ranking.
- Hear your own intuition concerning the best options.

5. Recommendation

Finally, it is now possible for the problem solver to take the analysis to those who must approve it or provide resources to make it happen. This means the following actions are required.

- Prepare the ground with the approvals players.
- Describe the process you have been through.
- Set out the problem, the implications, the scale.
- Set out the success criteria for a solution.
- Set out the top three options, quantified, using the success criteria.
- Set out your recommendation from the three.
- Justify your recommendation.
- Seek approval based on the above.

It is remarkable how rarely this straightforward approach is taken, not only in assessing public sector problems but in presenting potential solutions to decision-making individuals or committees. Most intelligent people have a smart-alec tendency: if presented with a decision paper proposing only one solution to a problem, they will go out of their way to identify alternative options, thereby undermining the strength of the recommendation and pushing out the decision.

The effective public sector manager ensures that the non-executive or elected member is given a clear enunciation of the problem, a comprehensive set of options – and, implicit in the way these are set out as well as explicit in the recommendations at the end, a very clear steer as to which is the right road to take.

But it's the options bit that is often – usually – neglected; resulting in decision makers taking sometimes perverse or obstructive decisions *just to assert their right to do so.*

25. Three Rules of Public Sector Performance

In the private sector there is a very clear principle at the heart of performance management which is this. Focus. Focus on the activities which give you the best results. Ensure you know where your results are coming from. Do more of this and less of the stuff that's not working.

This works because the private sector, in the end, has a common currency – a simple means by which any activity can be compared with any other – called financial return on investment. If the investment made in any product, activity, service or member of staff does not produce a return in the form of increased profit, it should not be continued.

Though this sounds simple, in practice, of course, it is not. There are interdependencies between activities: selling cans of beans at a loss may bring customers into your shop who will then buy bread at a good margin. Profit cannot always be easily attributed to a particular product or service: how do I allocate the costs of the finance departments across the product range? Payback periods differ for different activities: there are risks and uncertainties. None the less, the principle is easily understood and underpins all good private sector management decisions.

The public sector does not have the luxury of a comparable approach. There is no common currency or scorecard allowing, for instance, the benefits of a hip replacement to be evaluated against a Maths GCSE. No calculation can be made which would show whether the nation would be better served by a pound spent on infertility treatment compared to a pound spent on higher education. Even within one department, the calculation is impossible: are heart replacements more worthy than impotence drugs?

This means that, though successful public sector managers must also focus on the important over the trivial, *it is much harder for them to identify exactly which is which*. Priorities will always be open to interpretation: "scientific" approaches to identifying leverage points and causalities always have a spurious feel to them and rarely result in sustainable performance benefits.

But focus remains important for the following reasons:

- Focus helps managers and staff cope with the often overwhelming set of responsibilities they are asked to carry. By clarifying key objectives or priorities, public sector leaders help bring a sense of coherence and meaning to the work of the organisations involved.
- The business of identifying points of focus, or priorities, if done properly (i.e. with and through the team as a whole), helps to build a sense of ownership and purpose; a sense that we are all working towards the same end.
- Some activities simply are more important than others and should be recognised as such, in spite of difficulties associated with proof. Children who are failed by their parents and their community in their early years, for instance, will be beyond the help of the education system as they approach their GCSEs. Where this failure is evident, it is more important that the main investment is made early. It is a key role for public sector leaders (wherever they sit in the organisational hierarchy) to identify and justify these leverage points.

So Public Sector Performance Rule 1 is:
Focus on the key leverage points.

But focus is not enough. In the education example above, we cannot simply allow ten years' worth of GCSE failure to happen until the early years interventions have been able to prove themselves. The private sector can (should?) close down non-essential or less important activities. The public sector does not have this luxury – for good reason. A school which has decided to become a specialist technology college cannot stop teaching English. A hospital which has developed a regional specialism in heart and lung treatment cannot easily stop its general surgery work.

So, in the main, the non-focus activity must be continued and it must be continued at an appropriate level. But it must not be allowed to take over too great a proportion of management time: time which is in short supply and which must be directed at the focus areas.

So Public Sector Performance Rule 2 is:
**Identify activity which is non-focus but has to be done
and *contain* it**

By contain I mean, define its budget and the management time it will be allowed. We will continue to offer vasectomies even though we want to establish our strongest reputation in heart and lung surgery. We will not claim any vasectomy high ground, but we will make sure what we do is at an acceptable standard and to budget.

But public sector activity is paid for by the public and is subject to considerable public scrutiny. And decisions where there should be focus and where there should be containment are highly sensitive. Everything is potentially under the microscope of public, ministerial and media scrutiny.

Rather than be passive in the face of this information assault, or hope that somehow it won't happen, the best approach is to take charge of the information flow. What is needed is a very clear understanding of the key audiences and stakeholders, and a well thought through, well implemented communications programme to ensure these groups feel that their needs and concerns are being taken into account: in short, that our work suits them, is justified in terms that they can understand, or – at least – is not indefensible.

This is *not* the same, of course, as telling them in simplistic terms what our focus/contain priorities are, since this will have the inevitable effect of alienating those (the majority, if we have done our focus thinking correctly) who have an interest in areas which we have not prioritised.

> So Public Sector Performance Rule 3 is:
> **Communicate, communicate, communicate**

It is a key job of all managers to listen and speak upwards and downwards within the organisation, with partners and wider stakeholders, and, most importantly, with the customer. In addition, speaking with the media is fundamental to the role of the most senior managers. If loyalty has been built throughout the organisation, there will be little danger of staff going off message. The best way to get staff to stick to the script is to have a script which reflects the truth and in which they believe!

26. Organisational Management: Keep it Real

Management Science and Stupidity

Universities fall over themselves to offer business degrees, MBAs and public sector MBAs. Everyone in work has a very clear opinion about the specific shortcomings of his or her manager. Yet it seems that public sector management is a weaker, less effective force than it was 50 or even 100 years ago. With all this management training around, how can this be?

Part of the answer lies in the Management Science concept itself: the supposition that management is about structures and processes, divorced from the particulars of the service or activity being managed; that the correct management approach to car manufacturing is essentially the same as to mental health support, or to social housing. But a car plant feels very different from a mental health centre, which feels quite different from a housing association. And so the management style must differ.

In addition, precisely because we have created these models of scientific management style, we have under-estimated the value of managers being on the job, meeting with customers, being involved in the detail of delivery; really knowing in detail and caring about how the task is done. People have management careers precisely because they won't have to get their hands dirty. Yet the managers we all respect are those who know more about how to do the job than we do – in the car plant as well as the hospital.

The fundamentals of managing an organisation for great performance are straightforward. They are simple to state and require great effort to make real. They are:

1. Know your organisation and your customer
2. Make good use of targets
3. Get your contract management right
4. Work with good people.

1. Know Your Organisation and Your Customer

The first requirement is for the manager to know, in detail, how the function or organisation does its work and adds value to the customer: what the core processes are, and who does them. In developing this understanding, there is no alternative to being on the shop floor regularly, frequently: *really getting the job under the skin*. There is also no alternative to reflecting continuously on what is learnt, drawing flow diagrams and bubble charts, mapping resources against need: thinking and re-thinking how the job activity could be improved. And this continuous improvement drive is also a never-ending task, in the awareness that perfection cannot ever be achieved but must always be sought.

What about processes and procedures? Make no mistake, procedures are necessary. They should specify broad parameters within which work should take place, and they should be explained properly to all staff. It is more usual for procedures to be over-detailed, restrictive and barely understood or followed by anybody. Less time spent on specifying policing and amending procedures means more management time walking the shop, ensuring procedures are being followed and resolving the nitty-gritty issues which the real world throws up.

I have seen plenty of public sector managers get by with hardly any grasp of what their function delivers, and have seen a good proportion of them promoted. Knowing your organisation and your customer is not critical to your career prospects. It *is* critical if you want to get things done.

2. Make good use of targets

Good management, amongst other things, involves setting targets and managing performance against those targets.

It is crucial that targets are simple and high level. It may well not be possible to specify organisational targets down to the level of each individual. What is more important is that each person has a sense of the direction of the organisation, and a sense of how they should contribute. This means that a very small number of headline targets or measures should be identified for the organisation as a whole, then managers should be given the responsibility for identifying (small numbers of) targets for individuals. Though it may be more reassuring for the top team to believe that the whole organisation has been engineered to have a strong Golden Thread of targeted accountability running through it, in reality this is almost never how things are (except, perhaps, in highly predictable environments, which are relatively rare in public service). *Better results are achieved where the senior team allows itself to live with more uncertainty.*

Again, this approach releases more management time for walking the shop floor and for getting involved in resolving the real situations that always occur and which can never be designed out.

This approach is not a soft alternative. Staff must be held firmly to account. But they should be held to account for their behaviour against a set of principles; values which explicitly state the organisation's commitment to customer service, fairness and getting things done. People – including managers – who do not live up to this value set should be got rid of as soon as possible; and managers should be held to account for this happening.

I have seen hospitals ruined and patients' lives lost because key staff hit targets but had the wrong values. I have seen committed and effective organisations get into trouble because their performance reporting systems were poor. The latter issue is easy to fix. The first, where a corrosive culture has developed, usually requires the organisation undertakes a wholesale rebuilding from the bottom up.

3. *Get your contract management right*
It is important to recognise that, for many parts of the public sector, contract management is a necessary core discipline. It should not be a Cinderella function, staffed by the most junior folk: it is where value is or is not added.

When people are looking for efficiencies, they rarely recognise that savings made in contract management usually end up being outweighed by inefficiencies resulting elsewhere in the system: by areas of ineffective delivery being hidden in amongst the wider activity set comprising a large contract; by higher rates demanded by overhead-heavy bigger businesses; or by unresponsiveness to the customer resulting from over-worked and out of touch contract management of the deliverers.

I am including commissioning and procurement under the contract management heading. These have become fashionable topics in the public sector. There is an emerging understanding in health, in regeneration, in skills and other areas, that third party delivery can add considerable value if it is specified and structured in the right way – a value much wider than the apparent core of the contract.

You can use public money to build new social housing, or you can use it to build new communities in which the house building has been used as the catalyst for investing in local construction skills, local employment in the construction process, local loyalty and social capital; as the basis for long term well-being, which correlates with better health, better education outcomes, and reduced economic vulnerability.

Primary health care commissioning can be done in a way which allows voluntary organisations to deliver health promotion programmes, for instance, or elements of mental health provision. The best of such organisations have deep roots in the community. By strengthening them, wider social bonds in the community are potentially strengthened, which results in greater levels of satisfaction with the area amongst the population and, as a consequence, better health and a wide range of socio-economic benefits.

All this is possible with **effective commissioning** – thinking about what you want; **procurement** – choosing it; and **contract**

management –agreeing on the detail and managing the on-going relationship.

Good contract management – contract management that maintains effective control but which also allows for responsiveness in the system – is possible. The answer is to *keep contracts simple*; to resource the contract management function so that there is *no bundling of activities* into bigger contracts; that there *is competition between contractors*, and that that *contract managers understand their job*, which is not only to police the paperwork but also to get close to the customers' experience of the service, and to specify the service in terms which include more than the obvious.

When a new building is to be constructed for public sector use, for instance, the contract can be specified in such a way that a good proportion of the money spent stays in the local economy (local contractors, local skills levels, etc). Public sector service contracts (non-medical services in hospitals, buildings maintenance, etc) can be specified to emphasise the importance of customer engagement. While this may not directly advantage the local supplier (which would be against EU legislation) it will at least ensure that local responsiveness is built in.

Finally – and here is the brutal bit – the worst 10% of service deliverers should not have their contracts renewed on a regular basis. The contract should make this specific in order to make it legally enforceable. Contract managers should be required to make it happen, and politicians should be helped to understand – in the face of the inevitable howls of complaint – why this is necessary if their policies are properly to be translated into practice. Done properly, there is no requirement that under-performers be identified according to 'objective' mechanistic measures or outputs. An across-the-board evaluation conducted by an independent panel which includes customer experiences is a valid approach.

4. Work with Good People

All organisations comprise 5% very effective people, 10% ineffective, and 85% adequate. The management task is to give the best people more influence, encourage and motivate the adequate people, and get rid of the ineffective.

The toughest part is to identify and get rid of the ineffective ones. Understandably, ineffective people often learn how to mask their ineffectiveness and learn how to make it difficult for managers to exit them. But unless they go, they have a negative effect on the rest of the team, since people generally have a well-developed (not always accurate) sense of who is not pulling their weight.

It is also important to watch the management hierarchy very carefully. Managers are not there to lord it over their staff. Their role is to help the front line deliver the service. It is a service role, paid well because it is hard and grubby. This means being there and helping. And it means celebrating – *celebrating success and celebrating where things have been tried, even if they have not succeeded.* The public sector continually attempts to identify and disseminate good practice. It usually fails because it is done in such a worthy fashion: dull reports are produced, dull conferences convened. But celebration is a great way of connecting with people's emotions in a way that lets the underlying facts into their consciousness.

There is nothing so corrosive to organisational effectiveness as a manager's failure to remove poor staff. It leads to all the other folk saying, "Why should I bother?" I remember speaking to a council Chief Executive I knew well, who had transferred from one council where he had been seen as a reasonably good performer, to another where his reputation was very quickly sky high. I wanted to know what had changed.

"Simple," he said. "There, the rules in my previous job meant I couldn't sack incompetent people. Here I can."

27. Financial Performance

Financial performance is a very different beast in the public sector. Unlike the private sector, where it is almost synonymous with performance, financial performance in the public sector can sometimes seem no more than an irritant or afterthought. I worked with a large city council in which resource allocation decisions were made by the Finance Director in complete isolation from political policy and operational management decisions. Much of the council's political and operational leadership was rendered irrelevant by this fact. In the end, the politicians and senior officers could say or write whatever they liked: if the Finance Director had not allocated a budget to their priorities, their priorities would not be progressed.

Outsiders will characterise the public sector as being a looking glass world in which spend is good and an unspent budget bad. This is simplistic. The reality is that both underspend and overspend are bad. What public sector organisations are required to do, in environments where demand (and indeed supply) are almost impossible to predict, is to hit their year end budget on the nail.

There are other challenges. Typically, the cash available for any activity, whether a new drug treatment or a new regeneration programme, is highest at the outset and declines (on an absolute and unit price basis) over time. Most activities (and public sector agencies) are fundamentally redesigned after five years and scrapped after ten. This is simply political reality: ministers or councillors need new announcements to be successful, so they are given generous budgets. But politicians also need (or feel they need) to announce a continual stream of new initiatives, so old programmes budgets are shaved to find the cash for the new. And elections happen on a three or five year cycle, resulting in the need (or the perceived need) for wholesale restructuring of public sector edifices in order to demonstrate to the electorate that brave decisions have been taken.

In addition, the public (or the media) does not take kindly to the misuse of public money. The newspapers glory in headlines about money spent on ridiculous projects or anti-social individuals; on quango chief executive salaries and overblown computer systems.

But very little public attention is paid to that enormous elephant in the public sector room: *the huge inefficiencies in many public institutions*. In recent years, a series of government-commissioned studies have examined the problem and proposed solutions, but they will only ever be optimised if the managers on the ground are prepared to bite the ethical and economic bullet and recognise that the nation's well-being overall depends upon robust financial management of our public sector activities, since this drives efficiency and effectiveness in the system as a whole.

How is effective financial performance achieved? There are six key elements.

- **Devolved responsibility, tight accountability**
  Give front line managers responsibility for their budgets within the constraints imposed by the funding received. Give them space to work out how best to achieve optimum results. Hold them to account for their performance in terms of (1) client impact; (2) conformance to (minimum) contractual requirements; and (3) budget spend.

- **Zero based budgeting**
  Don't roll budgets over year after year. Ensure that, every year, probing questions are asked concerning each line that makes up any individual's budget. On a regular basis – if not every year then every other year – take a zero-based approach: require each budget holder to justify why they should have any budget (including staff) at all. Force the organisation to review whether there are more effective ways of working.

- **Ruthless management of process non-conformance**
  Don't spend too much time on process design. Have processes that ensure conformance to your funding requirements and which support demonstrated good practice – but don't fall into the management science trap of thinking that new process manuals automatically result in improved activity. Remember the Hawthorne experiment (or look it up if you don't). But when you have defined processes (and few of us can avoid this) **police them hard**. If activity standardisation is important, then it's important enough to make sure it's turned into reality. For front line managers, process conformance should be key to the role – in the sense that they are there to make sure that people are able to do things well in support of the client and the mission.

- **Surplus management**
  To make a real difference in many public sector settings you need discretionary funds: main programme budgets are often so tightly defined and controlled that there is none of the latitude necessary to respond to client or project specifics.

  But discretionary funds are in short supply: ministers, Whitehall departments and the Treasury all need, or feel they need, high levels of centralised control. The trick is to procure discretionary funds by delivering mainstream programme outputs in such a way that a surplus is generated – which can then be used more imaginatively for related activity. There will be rules, of course, limiting the extent to which this is possible – and breaking those rules is not, in career terms, a sensible approach – but playing to the letter rather than the spirit of the rule is acceptable and often necessary. In order to generate funds from mainstream programmes you need to develop a clear, almost commercial, understanding of where the best margin lies, and to deliver high volumes of activity in that area (this is part of the **focus** point explored earlier in this section).

- **New programmes: Get in early**

  As we saw earlier, new programmes are usually generously funded. These are, therefore, potential sources of significant discretionary budget. To tap into the opportunity you need to be one of the early deliverers of the programme, preferably at the pilot phase. Ensure you over-deliver on the pilot phase outcomes and you will be generously rewarded with budget for the inevitable roll out. How do you arrange to be an early adopter? By playing civil service politics – by being seen as someone who will over-achieve, ensuring that the Minister's bright idea, which is being tested out, is shown to have been brilliant and worthy of full funding.

- **Flexible Projects**

  Given the unpredictable nature of most public sector environments, achieving 100% spend is well-nigh impossible without careful management. The standard device is virement: the transfer of budget between areas of over and underspend. This is a recognised budget management approach, though it is still seen as cheating by many, and will actively be proscribed in many settings or between significant budget lines. In the perception game of public service, too much budget virement can result in your being seen as a somewhat pedestrian operator, employing techniques which the funder may well allow (since all parties have an interest in hitting budget) but which are somehow not quite the done thing. The more sophisticated bureaucrat ensures that there is a range of legitimate, useful and wholly flexible projects either on the go or ready to go at short notice, where spend can be turned up or down at short notice, bringing forward planned activity from the subsequent year or pushing this year's activity out into next.

28. Basic Progress Tools

Basic Questions
The effective public sector entrepreneur never ceases to ask, and to seek to answer, the three basic strategy questions:

- Where are we?
- Where should we go?
- How do we get there?

Crucially, there must also be recognition that *these questions are not sequential*: the answer to one makes assumptions, or begs questions, about the others.

For example, if our current service is only meeting 10% of client needs (where are we now?), and we want it to address 100% of their needs (where should we go?), we will probably need more resources to make the change (how do we get there?). But in order to get those additional resources we will need to ask the "where we are now?" question with reference to a new set of issues: stakeholder relations, for instance; new funding options; or our financial management capabilities. The effective public sector entrepreneur holds all three questions in mind at once, recognising that robust understanding of current shortcomings is as important as building a compelling vision – as important as being pragmatic about what kind of progress is possible.

The boiled down messages we receive from Hollywood about success and enterprise – that you only need a dream compelling enough – are simplistic and juvenile. The real world is complex and contradictory; shades of grey, not black and white. Good enterprise understands and recognises the nitty gritty of the real world and works with the grain.

Where Are We?

When trying to get a comprehensive picture of the current state of affairs for their area of responsibility, good public sector managers use the following three viewpoints:

- **Responsiveness** (how responsive are we to customer and stakeholder needs?)
- **Efficiency** (what level of output do we produce for the inputs we receive?)
- **Innovation** (how effective are we at solving new customer, stakeholder or process problems, or finding better solutions to existing problems?)

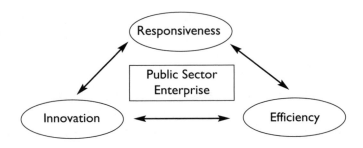

Collectively, these are a fair summary of organisational enterprise in the public sector.

There are no easy or scientific ways of answering any of these questions, of course. But the process of asking the questions, and of looking for ways of answering them, should lead to the improvements we seek under each heading.

Where Should We Go?

The three fundamental rules of public sector management were spelled out earlier. In summary, they are simply these:

- **Focus** (pick your priorities – a small number)
- **Contain** (ensure the non-priority areas do not become a problem)
- **Communicate** (find a way of ensuring you are on the front foot with stakeholders around these choices)

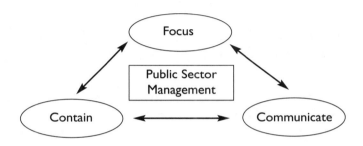

The answer to the question, "Where should we go?" must bite the bullet and identify priorities. Given the human capacity (or incapacity) to hold too many variables in one head at one time, the maximum number of priorities is probably six. This is what **focus** is all about.

How Should We Get There?

The two main checklists associated with progressing the "How should we get there?" question are: (1) stakeholder management; and (2) the basic change model. Effective stakeholder management identifies:

- Who we need to influence
- What we can offer that will be of use to them
- What we would like in return.

It generates a list of the key players, works out what the ask and offer is for each of them, then assigns responsibility either for making the approach or for finding a third party who can be ask/offered to do so.

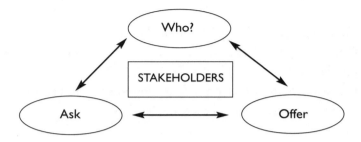

A basic but powerful change model says that real and sustained change will only work where the people involved experience three conditions:

- **Discomfort** with the current state of affairs
- **A compelling vision** of the new future
- **Clarity** concerning the first steps that should be taken towards that vision.

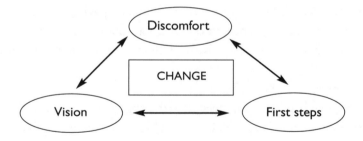

Effective public sector change ensures that the people who need to change feel all three. Unsurprisingly, given most people's desire to be nice to each other, the one that is often neglected is the first: people *must be helped to feel unhappy with the status quo.*

29. The Use and Abuse of Strategy

Vast amounts of public sector time are spent on the development and documentation of strategy. Very often the resultant documents gather dust while the organisations carry on with pretty much what they would have done anyway.

Strategy can make a positive difference. If it does not do so, we should not do it.

Strategy can be seen as being either **response** or **ritual**: a reaction to challenges in an organisational environment, or something we simply feel compelled to do by virtue of being human. Both explanations have validity – both approaches may have utility.

Strategy as Response

If there were no change, there would be no need for strategy: once an organisation had worked out how to do its job, it would simply carry on doing it.

But there is always change, there are always new challenges; organisations must continually respond and adapt. So why is strategy so often ineffective, out of step, or inappropriate to the real issues on the ground?

The key is to recognise that organisations face different types of challenge and that the response – both in terms of the strategy process and the management or leadership style – must be shaped accordingly. The way the world's leaders plan to respond to the news that a meteorite will hit the earth in six months' time should be different from the way they respond to the long term issue of global warming. In other words, good strategy and strategic leadership are **contingent** on the details of the challenge itself.

Challenges do not come neatly packaged with sticky labels identifying how best we should respond. But there are essentially four categories of organisational challenge, each of which requires a quite different strategic response. Working out which category applies in any given circumstance is, of course, itself a challenge.

Challenge	Key Strategic Response	Leadership Style
Multi-variable	Blueprint	Planning
Crisis	Speed	Authority
Chaos	Meaning	Cooperation/catalyst
Scale	Resources	Confidence

Multi-variable Challenges

When the challenge is complex – but essentially knowable – this is a multi-variable challenge. Large scale examples might be the building of an ocean liner, putting a man on the moon or opening a hospital. They have been done before; the component parts are well understood; they can be done again. Multi-variable challenges may be much more limited in scope for smaller organisations – moving offices, perhaps, or an organisational merger.

The key strategic response to this kind of challenge is to develop the equivalent of a blueprint or engineering diagram: we need a plan which specifies, in detail, what will be done when and by whom, and with what resources. The required leadership style is cerebral, thorough: plan-focused.

This is the default response and management style adopted across the public sector. Many would see this approach as being what proper strategy and leadership really are about – and, in the right circumstances, it works very well – but only in the right circumstances.

Crisis Challenge

We all know what a crisis looks like. When one of these hits, a thorough, logical, well thought-through response will usually be a luxury we cannot afford. By the time the response has been developed, the crisis has done its worst and the strategy is irrelevant.

The public sector deals with crises as part of its day job (major accidents, riots, infectious diseases), but here we are more interested in organisational crises which cannot be anticipated: major unplanned spending imperatives, media exposés, system failures, widespread corruption or audit failures.

The key strategic response is speed and decisiveness: often, it matters less *what* response is made to the crisis than that *any* response is made with conviction and energy. The required leadership style is therefore authoritative, decisive, even dictatorial.

It is not the norm, yet not unusual, to see this kind of approach to strategy and leadership adopted in public sector settings even when there is no crisis. Many people would characterise good leadership as being decisive and forceful – the Winston Churchill style of management. Many leaders would prefer to operate at the top of a hierarchy and make decisions on the fly than to be more thoughtful and inclusive. This approach has its place – when there is a war on, for instance – but crisis is not the only, or even the most common, challenge. However, when a comet is about to hit the earth, let's not fuss about making sure all parties are consulted on what colour we should paint the missile we intend to use to blow it up.

Chaos Challenge

A chaos challenge is one in which there is complexity, like the multi-variable challenge, but in which it is not possible to know all the details. There are many elements to be taken into account in building an ocean liner – but they can be listed, modelled and managed. But there is an infinite number of variables at play in, for instance, an economy. To generate economic growth in a UK region you cannot seek to itemise, model and oversee all the elements which may have an effect. This is called a 'chaos' challenge in recognition of the fact that the trend lines are unreliable; that what worked before may well not work again; that the solution is not only unknown, it is unknowable. A different response is required.

The trouble is that chaos challenges look a little like multi-variable challenges. Because the public sector system is uncomfortable with unknowables, it tries to condense the issues down to a set of variables that can be managed, and then to programme them. As a result, for instance, we get complex skills problems (a chaos challenge) being addressed through investment in NVQs (as part of complex, but essentially planned educational supply systems). NVQ achievement goes up, but the skills problem remains.

In chaos, the management style must encourage cooperation between all relevant parties: we are looking for on-going responsiveness to whatever the next day may bring. The leaders must be catalysts, helping the team to become a fluid, dynamic, motivated reactor. And the strategy? – the key strategy focus should be on creating **meaning**: on ensuring that the team have a common understanding and passion for what they are trying to achieve so that, whatever they choose to do, it will be in line with the overall mission.

Scale Challenge

Some challenges are so huge, in relation to what the organisation is usually charged with doing, that they require a significant step change in approach. These are scale challenges.

The correct leadership style is confidence: instilling in the team and in the wider stakeholder set a sense that this is sensible and doable – that it is not, in fact, as much of an extraordinary challenge as it first appeared. And the key strategic response focuses on capability and resources; on the amassing of the capacities required to raise the game.

Strategy As Ritual

Humans are planners. They differ from other animals in this respect: they are capable of thinking through possible future scenarios and how best to shape their behaviour to get what they want. This planning (strategising) activity is natural.

Not all natural behaviours are appropriate to immediate circumstances, of course. But, if we want to understand why people in the public sector do so much strategy, it is useful to understand that sometimes they simply do it because that is what people tend to do.

If we allow ourselves to think of strategy as ritual (which is not to say that it is only ritual, or always ritual – or even to imply that ritual behaviour cannot also be useful behaviour), then it may shed light on why it can sometimes be so counter-productive.

There are six varieties of strategy ritual.

	Approach	Activity
	Audit	*List existing activity*
	Logic	*Quasi-scientific alignment of needs against competences*
Ritual	Delay	*Do more research*
	Avoid	*Reframe the problem*
	Involve	*Discuss*
	Authority	*I am clever*

Audit Ritual

In this version, strategy is simply collating all accounts of existing activity in a single document entitled 'strategy', with dates demonstrating that it covers the coming three (or five or ten) years. Most often employed when a (quasi) partnership is creating a partnership strategy, this strategy ritual adds no value in itself but gives the participants a warm feeling about being in the same room together.

Logic Ritual

This is the most common version of strategy ritual; the one that feels like it is actually progressive and meaningful. An analysis of the problem to be solved is then cross-referenced to the resources and capabilities available; priorities are identified, targets set, and suggested re-structurings described. The resultant document is seductive, precisely because of this apparently seamless logical flow.

The logic ritual can be robust and useful, as it is intended to be. More often, the problem is described in such a way as to lead inevitably to the solution which had always been preferred (We need to invest in training to close the skills gap – We need to introduce an internal market into the NHS – We need to increase levels of respect amongst young people), leaving a compelling set of logic which does not solve the underlying problem. Or, rather more manipulatively, the authors of the document may hide within their flow a number of false logic steps – where the intervention (and the scale of intervention) suggested against a particular problem is either unproven, barely scratches the surface of the issue, or simply puts a sticking plaster over the real problems. Because the logical chain looks good, the proposed responses are approved – even when they may elsewhere be known to have been counter-productive (for instance, shock treatment in responding to gang violence).

Delay Ritual

The need to develop a strategy can be a useful approach for those who want to procrastinate – for good reasons or bad. It is hard to argue against the assertion that we need to know more about the challenges that face us before we take precipitate action. Indeed, those who advocate *doing rather than talking* can look impetuous, unsophisticated or even immature: not good career attributes in the public sector.

Avoidance Ritual

Similar to the delay ritual approach, the expressed need to develop – and be seen to develop – strategy can be a useful way of avoiding action altogether. By calling for a strategy in response to the challenges faced, the public sector manager may be hoping that the problem will solve itself, or progress into some other issue beyond his/her immediate responsibility; meaning that, when the strategy ritual is complete, there is no longer anything left to do.

Involvement Ritual

The strategy development process can (and often should) be a ritual in which stakeholders are brought together and forced to work together. The resultant documented agreement may be less important than the inter-personal connections which are built between individuals in the process; by the realisation that it is indeed possible to work with 'these people'.

Developing the strategy itself, therefore, can be less important than the way in which it is done: the venue where the meetings are held, the hospitality shown by the host; the deference shown to each other by the parties concerned.

Authority Ritual

It is not unusual for the strategy to be written in its entirety by one individual, usually the most senior. Consciously or not, the Chief Executive is saying, by doing this, "Look how clever I am!".

30. Projects, Organisations and Partnerships

Public sector management and leadership can be a complex game, requiring a wide variety of approaches depending on the environment and the particular management challenge. Broadly speaking, though, public sector heroes will find themselves managing and leading on three overlapping types of entity: **projects, organisations and partnerships**. The fundamentals of each of these three are quite different.

Managing Organisations

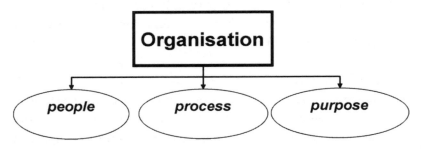

Effective public sector leaders and managers maintain three parallel perspectives on their organisation. These are:

1. How are my people doing? (people)
2. Are we achieving what we intended? (purpose)
3. Are we doing things the way we should? (process)

They put greater or lesser attention to each of these as dictated by current and future issues/opportunities.

People
All people in work are managers: we all have work relationships with other people that require attention. In managing others, a good

proportion of individuals have good **challenge** competences, holding people to account for good performance. A similar proportion have some **support** abilities, ensuring that the needs of individuals are met and that they are happy in and trained for their task. Few combine the two capabilities. Even fewer combine them with an ability to **inspire** – and knowledge of when to use the different management styles.

It is this, the ability to challenge, support or inspire the people you work with, and the insight required to know when to do which, that sets apart the excellent public servant.

Purpose

For human beings to enjoy their work, and to work most effectively, they need to feel part of a meaningful endeavour. The three competing perspectives which can give work meaning are:

1. wealth generation (for self or for others)
2. the development of the community (to which the individual belongs or for which they have strong feelings)
3. the protection of the environment (planet).

In the private sector, the second and third of these are often neglected, leading to a demeaning of the people in the business. In the public sector, the first and third of these can be ignored, leading to a sense of exploitation. The excellent public service leader maintains an effective balance between these three drives in shaping, monitoring and managing the business.

Process

In many organisations, prompted by the growth of the quality accreditation movement, some **analytical** thought has been applied to the flow of work. The vogue for business process re-engineering has had the benefit of reducing the amount of wasted activity. There is a danger that, on the way, **creativity** will be squeezed out of the system: there is little scope to try doing something a different way.

In addition, the cumulative, unconscious understanding that experienced people gain – their **intuition** – is frequently neglected in favour of predetermined choices based on out of date circumstances.

The excellent public service leader ensures that the organisation has absolute clarity concerning its core (analytical) processes – the fundamental and simple workflows that comprise its core functions. But he or she also ensures that those processes are specified and overseen in a way which allows flexibility: which encourages people to bring creativity to how they do what they do, and which allows for personality, engagement and intuition in seeing through their work.

Managing Partnerships

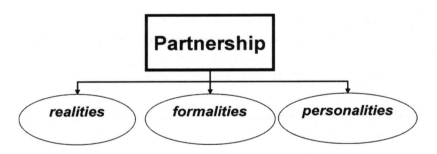

Public sector leaders must work with and through partnerships – with other functions or other agencies/businesses. Effective organisational leaders and managers maintain three parallel perspectives on partnership building and working. These are:

1. What do the key individuals need and want? (personalities)
2. What are the budgetary and bureaucratic niceties which may be served? (realities)

3. How do we constitute the partnership so that it is most effective? (formalities)

Personalities
The leader works hard to:

- identify the personal objectives (often unstated) of key players
- understand and use the words used by the key players
- keep enthusiasm up by delivering quick results.

Realities
Whatever the rhetoric of partnership, realities still lurk beneath; rocks just below the surface of a shifting sea of partnership. A good passage is made by the navigator who knows where the rocks are.
The main realities to concern us are associated with power:

- Who has the budget?
- Who has the information?
- Who has the ear of higher level stakeholders?

In addition, there will usually be history between at least some of the partnership players – old alliances or old enmities, deals to be honoured or broken. Knowing about, and playing the chess game of, these political issues is the very stuff of partnership progress.

What's more, though formal plans, organisation charts and budget management often have little to do with the realities of making progress on the ground, they will get in the way if they are not contained and addressed to the satisfaction of the resource owners who require them.

The effective public sector operator does what is necessary to be seen to give attention to these realities, but *does not allow them to substitute for meaningful progress.*

Formalities

The constitution of any partnership (committee membership, voting rights, election process, contracts) can take up an inordinate amount of time. In managing partnership projects, the public sector entrepreneur should not duck the constitution issue, should ensure that good and detailed work is devoted to it at the early stage, and should ensure that further debate is then closed off. *The key principle is that form should follow function.*

The buy-in of all key players (individuals) is critical to progress. There is no substitute for getting the key individuals publicly to state their unequivocal support for the project, for the particular resolution, project phase, whatever. People who make a public commitment will typically seek reasons to demonstrate why they were right to have done so, rather than seek reasons to undermine.

Partnership projects often fail because the right authority has not been obtained. This can be anything from formal approval for expenditure being passed through the correct sign-off committee or mechanism, through to a middle manager with considerable negative power feeling that her nose has been put out of joint as a result of not being consulted.

Good partnership management practice includes *identifying key authority mechanisms (hard and soft) at the early stage and managing them throughout.*

Managing Projects

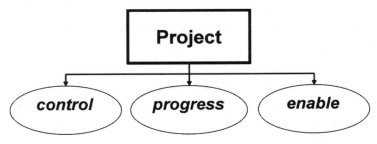

Increasingly, public sector leaders make progress in their working life through serial or parallel endeavours, assignments or projects, rather than through a career or through predictable process management roles. Project management skills are increasingly important in most roles. Effective organisational leaders and managers maintain three parallel perspectives on project performance. These are:

1. How do I keep this endeavour under control? (controlling)
2. How do I maintain momentum and buy-in? (progressing)
3. How do I keep the context supportive? (enabling)

Controlling
A project will have a clear and widely supported rationale, direction of travel, business case and resource allocation. It will have identified responsibilities, key milestones and risks.

A project will be controlled through stages, initiated and signed off at the top level. The original business case will be revisited at the inception of each stage.

A project will be formally concluded when its objects are achieved or when the original business case no longer stands. A lessons-learnt log will actively be maintained.

Progressing
Project stages will be identified, in outline terms, at the project outset. Their interdependencies will be identified and an overall schedule documented. The ability to chair a discussion, to elicit and progress key issues and priorities, is an important part of complex project management. No effective public sector player neglects the basic financials. Keeping track of cash and people (actual vs budget) is an essential skill.

Enabling
Effective public sector leaders are attuned to stakeholder management.

Making progress often means working with and through multiple stakeholders, usually with competing agendas. Progress is made by understanding, at the level of the individual stakeholder, the **ask** (what we want from them) and the **offer** (what we can give which meets their needs/wants).

The good public sector leader actively manages risks – the potential issues which may inhibit progress. Risks are clearly identified and recorded, and categorised by likelihood and impact.

The effective leader not only has financial competence: he or she employs that ability to good effect. Every endeavour has a budget and possibly a detailed profit & loss and cash flow statement for its duration.

31. The Mechanics of Problem Solving

We have explored how public sector actions, or interventions, can be seen as **transactions**; as services delivered by service providers to clients, who are characterised by their particular need for that service. Alternatively, any action can be seen as one of a series of actions which make up a **relationship** between two individuals, or between one individual (the citizen) and the various individuals who provide the service over time.

Or the action can be seen as part of a wider set of joined up actions which make up a wider set of relationships between a citizen and the various individuals who are employed by the public purse to help that citizen lead a more fulfilling and productive life.

The transaction-oriented approach results in a very different management style from a relationship-oriented, joined-up approach.

It is appropriate, efficient and effective for some services to be managed on a primarily **transactional basis**. The required management approach will be characterised by a target orientation, a 'masculine' management style, priorities based on analysis, and an emphasis on customer segmentation.

Services which require a more **relationship-based approach** are best managed with an emphasis on attitudes and values (more than targets), a 'feminine' management style, more space for intuition alongside analysis, and with more emphasis on what people have in common and how to connect them, and less emphasis on segmentation.

In truth, most public sector activities fall somewhere between the two and must be managed in a way which sees the service through both 'masculine' and 'feminine' eyes. In recent years the general culture has leaned too far towards the transactional: we need a rebalancing back towards the relational: recognising the importance of connecting with people (front line professionals, clients, etc) and sustaining that connection over time.

Different Needs, Different Responses

The public sector exists to support the needs of the citizen in a variety of ways. These needs may be complex or summarisable, or somewhere in between. A complex need is one that is infinitely variable and probably individual circumstance-specific – for example, the *particular* combination of individual and family circumstances which have led to a personal breakdown. A summarisable need is one that is reasonably consistent over different individuals: for example, the need for exercise.

Needs may also be fast changing or consistent over time. An example of a fast changing need might include gang culture (where gang behaviours and power positions are highly fluid). Slower changing needs include housing: we all need somewhere to live.

Our response must reflect these characteristics. The Needs/Response table below sets out the broad types of response required.

Table 1: Needs/Response Matrix

	Mainstream Services	Task and Finish Teams
Summarisable needs	*Scientific Model*	*Guerrilla Model*
Complex needs	Cross-functional Working	Neighbourhood Management
	Professional Peers Model	*Bonding and Bridging Model*
	Slow changing needs	**Fast changing needs**

Much of the public sector behaves as if all needs can be met through a **mainstream services-style solution** (the top left box). This is characterised by:

- a data-rich, scientific planning model,
- an emphasis on process compliance,
- a hierarchical management style oriented towards performance indicators and efficiency.

This is the **transactional approach** described in the previous section.

However, many of the toughest challenges we face are not amenable to a transactional approach, but fall into one of the other three categories. So different perspectives, skills and interventions are needed.

Faced by a challenge, our first task is to assess where it sits on the summarisable/complex spectrum, and on the slow/fast changing spectrum. This will locate the issue in one of the four boxes. It is then straightforward to know what the basics of the response should be.

So, for instance, let's look at an infection control issue in a hospital. It's summarisable (an infection control issue) and fast changing (we don't know how it's going to progress from day to day. So it belongs in the top right box. This means that we need a Guerrilla model response – that is, an autonomous team (or teams), made up of people with experience and expertise, who are empowered to make decisions and take action to contain and design out the problem. This management structure is usually called, in the public sector, a Task and Finish team.

Let's take another example. There is a long running problem between two communities in a particular area. The history of antipathy between them has created its own myths and scar tissue; it is continually boiling over into minor tensions and, occasionally, really serious incidents. The causality is a complex mix including cultural misunderstandings, personal vendettas going back generations and unscrupulous exploitation by criminal elements. So it's complex and fast changing, because the problems can manifest themselves in a wide and unpredictable variety of ways. It therefore belongs in the bottom right box. It requires a Bridging and Bonding response; a real and long term investment in building stronger relationships between influential individuals of all ages within and across the communities. The appropriate public sector intervention is usually called Neighbourhood Management, though the issue need not be about specific geographies, and the solution really is not about management but about empathy – good neighbourhood managers know this.

The bottom left box – where the needs are complex but slow changing – is where a Professional Peers model is required. The intricate and interwoven needs of a badly 'dysfunctional' family, for instance, do not respond well to a silo-based public service delivery approach. Is the problem a truancy problem, for instance, or child abuse, or domestic abuse, or substance abuse? Although there may be a series of crises, the basic patterns of the issue do not greatly change from month to month (or, in some cases, from generation to generation, if the intervention is ineffective). A service-by-service analysis-and-planning response to the issue will simply fail to respond in a way which takes the whole issue into account. What we need is to allow the front line professionals (education, social services, health, police etc) to bring their professional support and intuition to bear at the same time as connecting with each other as a set of individuals. The management task is to create the space and the culture in which this can happen. This is **Cross-Functional Working**, and is best managed by giving front line people the space and support to work it out for themselves on a case by case basis, rather than by trying to design an over-prescriptive process they must follow. A checklist or process-oriented approach will tend to get in the way of the inter-personal, inter-professional relationships which are fundamental to a successful outcome.

The table below sets out a more detailed picture of this analysis.

Table 2: Needs/Response Matrix in detail

	Slow-changing needs	Fast-changing needs
Summarisable needs	**Demand**: predictable **Solution**: professional service **Management focus**: standards, efficiency **Informed by**: objective data **Planning focus**: information and analysis	**Demand**: observable **Solution**: focused responsiveness **Management focus**: issue specific, task and finish **Informed by**: some objective data + relationship-based intelligence **Planning focus**: project parameters set by corporate, team flexibility within these
Complex needs	**Demand**: individual by individual, recognisable patterns **Solution**: multi-disciplinary around the individual **Management focus**: response framework, professional relations **Informed by**: individual narratives **Planning focus**: case by case	**Demand**: multiplicity **Solution**: peer support, plus acting as advocate for improved services **Management focus**: working with community catalyst **Informed by**: networks and friendships **Planning focus**: planting seeds, nurturing, pruning

32. The Characteristics of a Public Sector Hero

How can we recognise an effective public sector entrepreneur?

Luckily, there is no standard type. Public sector enterprise is pursued by a wide variety of people, often those who might seem the least likely, the most risk-averse, the most bureaucratic. Indeed, their very greyness can be the perfect camouflage in a system which does not encourage innovation.

There are, none the less, a number of characteristics by which the best can be identified – or even helped to develop. These we have listed under two headings: (1) **outlook** and (2) **action**. It is unlikely that any one person possesses all these characteristics. But you should find it a helpful checklist.

The Outlook of a Public Sector Hero

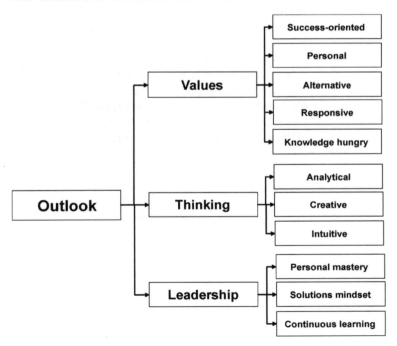

Values

Public Sector entrepreneurs are people whose hearts are in the right place – who want to make things happen, want to connect with their fellow man, want to keep developing themselves. The SPARK mnemonic (Success-oriented, Personal, Alternative, Responsive, Knowledge-hungry) encodes those human values that are the foundation on which personal public service capability is built.

Success-oriented

A Public Sector entrepreneur recognises the importance of:

- Results
- The celebration of results
- Bringing energy and enthusiasm to what he/she does.

Personal

A Public Sector entrepreneur recognises the importance of:

- Other people's feelings
- Actively listening to other people's feelings
- The ability to manage his/her own feelings in the face of the actions and feelings of others.

Alternative

A Public Sector entrepreneur recognises the importance of:

- Being true to him/her self
- Looking for answers beyond the obvious, however unfashionable
- Paying close attention to the language that is used, as well as the apparent content of that language
- Finding common ground between conflicting viewpoints.

Responsive

A Public Sector entrepreneur recognises the importance of:

- Shaping action in the light of needs
- Taking risks and making decisions
- Taking a lead, and matching the leadership style adopted to the circumstances.

Knowledge-hungry

A Public Sector entrepreneur recognises the importance of:

- Space for thinking
- Maintaining a curiosity about the world
- Finding and maintaining varied sources of information
- Looking for patterns, using and rejecting analogies.

Thinking

Public Sector entrepreneurs possess good mental equipment. They use their minds as fundamental tools of their trade, recognising the variety, strengths and shortcomings of a range of cognitive processes. They need to have an **analytical** ability: the ability to dissect a situation; to understand the underpinning skeleton or causal map. They must also be able to bring **creativity** to the process of looking for solutions; they must be good at identifying patterns and parallels which can elucidate possible answers. In addition, they must be able to listen to their own **intuition** and have respect for the intuition of others concerning what is real, what is possible, and what is most likely to work.

Analytical

The Public Sector Entrepreneur works hard to dissect, itemise and categorise the multiple inter-woven issues and characteristics of their complex environment. They use their brains to identify or postulate the fundamental skeleton which gives primary shape to the presenting situation.

Based on this disaggregation, the Public Sector entrepreneur then works hard to identify patterns linking the component items: causal links or correlations which have a familiar shape, based on personal or third party experience.

Creative

The Public Sector Entrepreneur uses comparable patterns to explore possible solutions, trends or dangers; to identify how the situation may progress without and with intervention. But he or she does not assume that the pattern, parallel, analogy or metaphor is correct: it is recognised as being a useful mental construct rather than an inevitable predictor.

The Public Sector Entrepreneur recognises that the language used to describe a situation can narrow the possible options explored for progressing it. Engineering-based language and imagery may lead to sub-optimal structural solutions; systems-based language may lead to ineffective process-oriented solutions; organic metaphors may lead to social or emotional responses. The Public Sector Entrepreneur looks at the situation from all three perspectives.

Intuitive

The Public Sector Entrepreneur recognises the wealth of experience, of parallel patterns, of insight which may be stored in the subconscious brain. He or she does not limit thinking to conscious, logical, front-of-brain approaches but gives time and listens to his or her intuition. The Public Sector Entrepreneur does not let intuition rule the actions taken, but does act carefully when doing so counter-intuitively.

Leadership

Personal Mastery

Public Sector Entrepreneurs seek out critical feedback, understand their own limitations and work to address them. They work with others who have complementary profiles. Public Sector Entrepreneurs pause before reacting emotionally. Public Sector Entrepreneurs, above all, take responsibility for their own lives, for their actions, for the contribution they make to their world.

Solutions Mindset
Public Sector Entrepreneurs are interested in answers. They investigate issues, but only to help resolve them. They have the energy and the charisma to identify and build solutions, bringing people with them.

Continuous Learning
Public Sector Entrepreneurs know that to stay curious is to stay alive. Public Sector Entrepreneurs celebrate when their assumptions are challenged.

Public Sector Entrepreneurs place mental and physical maintenance high on their priority lists.

The Actions of a Public Sector Hero

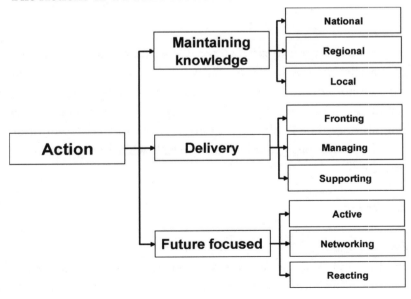

Maintaining Knowledge

In all sectors, information is power. Effectiveness is significantly impaired by out of date information, lack of familiarity with policy developments, or the use of outdated words. Public Sector Entrepreneurs work hard to maintain and *extend their knowledge base*, to stay abreast of strategy or policy debate and political fashion, and to employ contemporary vocabulary. They maintain a particular familiarity with the issues and developments in a specific area, with which much of their work may be associated, though they also keep an eye on general developments and trends.

National and International Level

A Public Sector Entrepreneur maintains an *awareness of the national and global competitive environment* or, in the public sector, the government departmental personalities and policies, key programmes and agencies.

Regional

Public Sector Entrepreneurs have *an understanding of the competitive environment at the sub-national level* or, in the public sector, the principal regional agencies and mechanisms, their inter-relationships, the key personalities (both executive and non-executive), and the key programmes plus associated funded constraints.

Local

Public Sector Entrepreneurs don't allow their wider knowledge and techniques to obscure the fact that, when progress happens, it happens locally, it happens individual by individual. They work hard to maintain and grow *personal connections* with their target customers, and with those who work directly with them.

Delivery

Public Sector Entrepreneurs are people who, in the end, *make things happen.* This, the unfashionable part – being so much more grubby and compromised than strategy or policy development, target setting or evaluation – is, in the end, the only thing that counts.

Rarely are Public Sector Entrepreneurs able to do it alone. Others – willing and competent or otherwise – are usually a necessary part of the team, function, partnership or loose alliance necessary to making progress. Public Sector Entrepreneurs work with the other individuals, assuming the optimum role required by the task and the nature of the team rather than the role they might prefer to play.

Fronting
Public Sector Entrepreneurs take *public responsibility* for a project or area of work; hold themselves, and the team, to account for its progress; are seen to be accountable; and actively seek out opportunities to raise the profile of the work, where so doing helps to make progress.

Managing
Public Sector Entrepreneurs not only know the techniques associated with project, partnership and organisational management, they also put them into practice. In addition, they *reflect* on their practice, looking for shortcomings and identifying potential areas of improvement.

Supporting
Public Sector Entrepreneurs are *not egotists*. When necessary, they are able to work as members of a team, supporting the managing and fronting individuals for the sake of the greater good.

Future Focused
Public Sector Entrepreneurs, as individuals, *take responsibility for their lives*. They invest in the process of progressing their lives and the development of their own experience. They recognise, if they have talent, that their talent should be nurtured and given full opportunity

to provide service to others; that talent is an asset which should be used to the full for the benefit of the many. They also accept that others will need to be convinced of the role that they play; that it is the process of convincing others which plays a part in developing and improving their talent.

Active
Public Sector Entrepreneurs *continually look for opportunities to use their talent*. They seek customers, allies and people, agencies or organisations that might support possible projects. They work hard to understand their own strengths and how to communicate them.

Networking
Public Sector Entrepreneurs *connect with people*. They seek to develop connections with interesting and influential people; they maintain those connections; they look for opportunities to help those people with their objectives in an unconditional way.

Reacting
Public Sector Entrepreneurs don't expect to plan everything in their lives. They are *open to suggestion*; they are open to opportunities that come their way. Public Sector Entrepreneurs are able to prioritise, to assess when an opportunity is worth pursuing and to clear the time and resource necessary to doing so.

PART SIX

CONCLUSION

When the public sector experienced its major growth, during the twentieth century, the emphasis was on process; on how to get the mechanisms of health, social welfare, education, functioning effectively and efficiently in support of the common good.

Over the decades since, the politicians have not lost their interest in tinkering with the systems and processes which make up public service, even though there is little evidence that politicians are best placed to oversee the mechanisms themselves.

In addition, there has been a necessary additional focus on purpose; on clarifying what the services are there to achieve and how success can be measured. Recent mantras have focused on targets and management. This new focus was an inevitable development: the clarity of purpose which was there at the outset had become less clear as a wider range of services became possible and the country became more sophisticated in its understanding of public service, less grateful for receiving any support at all, and more consumerist in its attitudes. But the central challenge of twenty first century public service is no longer principally about **process** or **purpose**. The new challenge is the **people** challenge. The early architects of the public sector could make assumptions about the behaviour of people which are no longer valid. The welfare state was, largely unconsciously, built on foundations which used as their cement a set of assumptions about the way people behave. Tinkering with workflow mechanisms (quality management, process mapping, organisational structure, etc) and purpose (targets, performance related pay, etc) can distract, and has distracted from, the essential moral endeavour, and from the natural behaviours that follow from it.

When management paraphernalia is built on top of the core task, the essential moral simplicity of public service is lost under the weight of conformance. Too often, broad brush prescriptions imposed on public service from the political or managerial centre require the front line worker to choose between (1) doing the right thing and being criticised or disciplined, or (2) following procedure even at the expense of the client. It is perhaps unsurprising that often he or she will choose the second. It is also unsurprising that, eventually, people become disillusioned, and begin to lose the ability to recognise the opportunity to do what ought to be done. We see this trend, caused by the understandable desire to impose consistent quality standards from above, across all parts of the public sector.

What is the great benefit of consistency? Surely the evidence of human existence, including that of the great twentieth century political movements, is that vitality and quality emerge most powerfully where there is vying and variety? Yet we petulantly demand sameness in public service: we decry the "postcode lottery" which is seen to result in poorer services in some areas.

It is not clear that a consistently poor service is a better option than a service which is poor in some areas and good in others – yet this is the choice. There is no evidence to say that the clarion cry of "best practice sharing" has any resonance in the human breast. Has anybody actually found a way to motivate people to share the best practice they have discovered?

There is good quality evidence to suggest that the way that people form and maintain personal and professional relationships is now quite different from when the welfare state was founded. We are less community minded, more isolated from each other, less inclined as individuals to feel a compelling responsibility to the welfare of our fellow citizens. We simply are not as good at supporting each other as we were before the age of television, personal transportation, computer games, materialism and the internet. People are now less likely to enter public service out of a sense of vocation and a desire to serve, and more likely to do so because it represents (relative) employment security. Health, social services, education and most other elements of the public sector were designed on the assumption that the fundamental means of delivering work were the employees, and that they cared. But people are not as good at caring as they once were. And the new paradigm is different: the (erroneous) belief is that the new fundamentals are not the people but the systems (which the employees serve); systems designed to make staff function more predictably and efficiently.

We are automating the workflows we have identified from the best functioning organisations. But the fact is that these systems cannot deliver the whole result without the **care** which used to come with the people who did what they did from a sense of service. Since care cannot be measured and quantified, we have left it out of the systems. And so the care dies. The systems function efficiently but the people fall between the cracks. Hospitals are under-cleaned. People are trained for jobs that don't exist. Abused children are visited but die anyway. Police forces improve their detection rates but communities remain terrified.

This should not suggest that we drop what we have learnt in terms of systems, processes and organisational management, nor that we should cease to employ targets and clear lines of accountability in order to provide public sector focus. But it does suggest that we need to allow people-based approaches back into the way we work.

What does this mean in practice? What it means is that we must stop trying to ape the private sector in our obsession with targets, process-design and efficiency – or, to put it another way, if we are to learn from the private sector, we should try to learn the whole story. Any successful commercial business takes as its starting point the need to satisfy the customer. Systematic efficiency must be subsidiary to, or parallel to, that aim. The public sector acts as if it were the worst sort of monopolistic megalith: it has forgotten that it must still "win" customers (we call it "engagement" and talk of "hard to reach groups" but it comes to the same thing). In our obsession with control and targets, the public sector's purpose can cease to be genuine progress for the citizen. The main objective for too many in the public sector is the production of information, which is sucked in by government and used to justify its continued position in power.

We should think of citizen relationships – customer engagement – as being assets with long term value; assets to be managed, developed and enhanced over time. Better public health does not result from a series of unconnected ten minute sessions in a GP's surgery. Improved business performance does not result from a one-off diagnostic transaction with publicly funded Business Link. Better education outcomes do not happen as a result of a test. Improved parenting does not happen as a result of a single improved parenting workshop.

If we were to adopt the better approach, a 'balance sheet' approach if we must use the private sector analogy, then we would structure our organisations, their internal management approach, their systems and their change management over time, around the maintenance of these relationship assets.

We would ask front line people to build, maintain and develop relationships.

We would ask managers to ensure that this happened – and to do so in the only real way possible, by getting out and seeing the relationships working in practice. We would recognise that output targets are still valid management mechanisms, but see them for what they are – no more than proxy indicators of the strength of the relationships being developed: useful but partial indicators of progress requiring substantiation by face to face review.

And we would ask senior managers to ensure that resource slack was built into the approach to allow for the relationship flexibility that will give our professionals the space to react early to emerging issues and forestall later crises.

We would put renewed emphasis on training and, specifically, on the facets of training which encourage and require personal responsibility, the ability to recognise a moral imperative, and the necessity to balance efficiency and responsiveness.

We would act quickly and robustly to dismiss those colleagues who abused the increased trust we would be putting in them.

We would find that we were doing the job more efficiently.

We would, in short, be revitalising the ethos of public service, releasing public sector enterprise: allowing the citizen and the public service heroes to take centre stage.